reaching
for the
canopy

Kylie Bullo was born in Kalgoorlie, a mining town in Western Australia renowned for its red dust. Her family headed to Victoria when she was a toddler and she soon had her first orangutan encounter at Melbourne Zoo. It was love at first sight.

It was not until her university degree that Kylie realised she had perhaps left the red dust of Kalgoorlie all those years ago to work with her real passion – the red apes! Kylie's world now revolves around orangutans and she has been the senior orangutan keeper at Perth Zoo since 2001. While she works with captive-bred orangutans, she also works tirelessly to prevent their extinction in the wild. She has extensive knowledge of and experience in the care and management of orangutans, including husbandry techniques, captive and wild behaviour, ecology and diet, reintroduction and release. Kylie was the keeper in charge of the world's only two zoo-born orangutans to be released into the wild. This involved years of planning and preparing the orangutans to be able to make the transition and adapt to jungle life.

Kylie has been the conservation project manager for The Orangutan Project (TOP) since 2005. TOP is a not-for-profit organisation providing funds for orangutan conservation, rainforest protection and education programs. It also supports the reintroduction of orangutan orphans into the wild in order to save the species from extinction. She has spent considerable time in the field in Sumatra and Borneo, working with and assisting orangutan conservation and rehabilitation projects.

Kylie Bullo

reaching
for the
canopy

UWA PUBLISHING

First published in 2015 by
UWA Publishing
Crawley, Western Australia 6009
www.uwap.uwa.edu.au

ISBN: 9781742587615
A full CIP data entry is available from the National Library of Australia

Cover photograph by Derek Smith
Typeset in Bembo by Lasertype
Printed by Lightning Source

For Temara, my fiery red-headed friend,
and to everyone who helped with her journey into the wild.

Temara contemplating her new forest home
(Photo: Peter Pratje)

CONTENTS

CONTENTS

FOREWORD

The book *Reaching for the Canopy* tells the story of two remarkable females, one human, one orangutan. Temara is the orangutan. Kylie Bullo, author of the book, is the human.

Temara was a captive-born orangutan at the Perth Zoo in Australia who undertook an extraordinary journey from captivity to freedom in the wilds of Sumatra. Kylie Bullo, a keeper at Perth Zoo, is the determined woman who helped make Temara's journey possible.

Kylie Bullo's dedication to orangutans is such that, when offered a keeper's job at Perth Zoo after university or undertaking a full fellowship for a PhD, Bullo did the unthinkable. She chose the zoo keeper's job and never regretted it. The book is serious about conservation. Bullo's wonderful sense of humour and good nature make it that oft-proclaimed phenomenon, "a fascinating read". Once or twice, I laughed out loud. However, Bullo's tribulations in Sumatra give the book heft and very much illustrate the difficulty of working and surviving in Sumatra's teeming (with insects!) tropical rain forests. A good sense of humour, as Kylie Bullo illustrates, always helps.

Orangutan Temara is an outstanding individual in her own right. Charismatic, sometimes obnoxious (or as obnoxious as an orangutan can be), rarely cowed, she is her own person with strong opinions of her own. Yet she can also be sweet and loveable. Independent-minded, stubborn and sometimes unpredictable, she was well chosen for the historic role she plays: the first zoo-born orangutan to ever return to the wild.

Kylie Bullo bares a part of her soul in telling us about her joint journey with Temara back into the forest where Temara's grandmother was born. The story of these two determined, passionate individuals, Temara and Kylie, who made zoological and conservation history, deserves to be read by anyone who has an interest in orangutans and great apes as well as primate conservation. Both Kylie and Temara blazed a path that others can follow.

The Perth Zoo needs to be congratulated on its enlightened view that captive animals can return and thrive in the wild.

Biruté Mary Galdikas

Dr. Galdikas with orphaned infant orangutan – Orangutan Foundation International

PROLOGUE

I pleaded with Temara to stop but she wouldn't listen. What had started out as a pleasant day in the forest had suddenly turned into a nightmare. The forest was very dry and there was a constant drone of bees in the air as they searched for water. My workmate Perizal and I had warned Temara about going near the bees, but she had a sweet tooth, so once she found a hive she couldn't resist trying to steal some honey. Before we knew it, Temara was being chased and stung repeatedly by a swarm of angry bees. We didn't want to be separated in the forest, so Perizal and I raced after Temara to try to help. Temara was never one for running, but she was naturally fast and, with the incentive of a swarm of bees after her, she ran like the wind.

We could barely keep up with Temara, and then the angry swarm seemed to grow as the bees turned their focus onto us. I fell further behind as I was stung repeatedly on the face and head. Perizal was faster than me and I begged him not to lose sight of Temara as she headed for a steep ravine to escape the bees. I had known Temara for seven years. She was only fourteen and she was my responsibility, so I couldn't lose her in a strange forest. I could barely see as I stumbled down the ravine to try to keep up with my companions. The stings pierced my skin and felt like stabbing hot needles. As I reached the river, I copied Perizal and dived under the water to escape the relentless stinging bees. The few seconds of relief we found were dashed by the realisation that Temara had disappeared. I bit my lower lip to try to stop it quivering. I tried to blink away tears but my body started convulsing with sobs from the pain of the bee stings and of not knowing where Temara had gone. I stood up in the river, scanned my surroundings and desperately screamed, 'Temara, where are you?' The silence was deafening.

Perizal and I began frantically climbing up the other side of the deep ravine in the direction we had last seen Temara. My legs felt like jelly as I struggled to keep up with Perizal, who moved further and further ahead of me. My face was quickly swelling from the poison, and my hands were bleeding from clasping onto whatever I could find to drag myself up the ravine. As my vision became blurred, I thought to myself, 'How the hell did I get into this mess?'

1

Pets galore

I can't lie and pretend that I loved orangutans and had dreamt of working with them since I was a little girl. In fact, my real passion for great apes only really took hold when I was at university. I was, however, born with the 'animal gene', as I call it – when someone has no possible path in life other than working with animals. My parents saw this in me from when I was four years old and tried to catch bees in the backyard because I thought they were cute and I loved them dearly. I wouldn't even be angry with the bees if I got stung.

Now, my parents were smart people and knew that lots of young children beg their parents for a pet only to become bored with it, and then poor neglected Fido has to be looked after by the parents, who never really wanted Fido in the first place! So they decided to test the waters and applied for our family to look after a guide-dog puppy for twelve months from the Lady Nell

Seeing Eye Dog School in Victoria. Puppies need to be one year old before they can commence their official guide-dog training, so suitable people are chosen to look after the puppies for this early period. My parents were successful in their application, and soon after a bouncing bundle of puppy love named Tracy entered our household when I was four years old. I loved Tracy! My memories of her are mainly days spent in the local park covering her in autumn leaves that had fallen to the ground. I also remember Mum following strict recipes from the Lady Nell School for Tracy and cooking her fancy dinners, including stewed meats such as tripe, and cooked vegetables. Unlike most families that have a dog, in our household, the important guide-dog puppy ate first and then the humans ate. Our time with Tracy ended far too quickly, but my parents felt that we had given her a fantastic start, with lots of love, before she entered the new stage of her life with guide-dog training.

After having Tracy, my parents agreed that my older brother, Michael, and I could have some permanent pets. My choice was a kitten. I was adamant that it would be named Fluffy even if it was nothing of the sort. I was so excited on the morning we went to the pet store to pick out our new family member. I chose a gorgeous little black kitten but was then told that the black kitten had already been sold and was being picked up the next day. I was quite upset but I wasn't leaving without a kitten, so I chose a little female grey tabby. I had my Fluffy. There was just one problem. Fluffy didn't like me. In fact, Fluffy didn't really like anyone. I think she must have had a traumatic kitten-hood, since she was extremely shy and nervous around people. So my dream of having a cuddly, fluffy kitten to love didn't really turn out as I had hoped. When I look back now, though, I'm horrified at some of the things Michael and I did to poor Fluffy in our desire to cuddle her. It's no wonder she didn't really like us. When Fluffy hid behind the washing machine to get away from us, Michael and I would leave a trail of kibble that led into the main laundry room, where we would hide behind the door so Fluffy couldn't see us. As soon as Fluffy came out from behind the washing machine to eat the kibble, we would pounce on her and pick her up for cuddles she did not want!

Michael was also allowed to have a pet. He chose a tortoise and called him Tortie – neither of us was very original when it came to naming our pets. Tortie had a large aquarium but we would also let him out in the backyard regularly for exercise. Michael and I used to have races with Tortie. We would put him at one end of the backyard, about 5 centimetres away from our 'finish line'. To win the race all Tortie had to do was stick his neck out over the line. Giggling, Michael and I would run to the other end of the yard and I would sit in a wheelbarrow. On the count of three Michael would push me in the wheelbarrow to the other end of the yard and across the finish line. We beat Tortie every time. A couple of years later a beautiful mohair rabbit named Sniffles joined the mix. Sniffles also had to endure our love; along with Fluffy, his least favourite game was probably being dressed up as characters out of our favourite cartoon, *He-Man*.

Of course I would never own a cat now and not have it sterilised, but back then we didn't get Fluffy 'done'. So when I was seven years old, Fluffy the cat became a fat cat: she had fallen pregnant to the street's resident fluffy, posh Persian cat. On my eighth birthday I contracted German measles. I had my two best friends over for a sleepover at the time so when I woke Mum in the middle of the night and showed her my all-over body rash, I was put into immediate quarantine. Of course I had to stay home from school, and I was promoted to rest in Mum and Dad's 'big bed' during the day and was fussed over by my mum. Fluffy decided to join me on the bed as well. On the third day of being in my parents' bed with me, she began to make funny noises. I called to Mum, who was in the other room, but she was watching TV and told me to wait a minute and she'd be there. (She was probably sick of me whining about being itchy.) After another few minutes Fluffy began to pant and I yelled out to Mum, 'Muuuuuuum, something black is coming out of Fluffy's bottom'. Mum arrived in the bedroom in about 0.3 seconds, wide-eyed and breathing heavily. She grabbed Fluffy and ran with her down the passageway and into the laundry, with a kitten hanging out! Fluffy was put in her luxury basket just in time to give birth to three divine kittens, two girls and one boy. I was quite upset while Fluffy gave birth because she was meowing loudly in discomfort and I couldn't do anything to help.

We gave the two female kittens to two of my friends from school and we kept the lovely little boy, which we called Timmy. Timmy took after his long-haired Persian father, so now I finally had the fluffy, friendly kitten I had always wanted. He was also a very loving and affectionate cat, since he grew up with us. For the next eleven years, though, I would always face the annoying question: 'Why is your non-fluffy cat called Fluffy and your fluffy cat called Timmy?' I would respond with, 'Because I was four when I named Fluffy even though she wasn't fluffy and then she had it off with a Persian and so her kitten was fluffy. It's not my fault!'

From the time we had Tracy as our first pet, I have never been without an animal. I just feel empty without having pets on whom to shower my animal affection. All my dreams came true when I was at university and my parents finally caved and said I could have a dog. It only took until I was about to leave home for them to say this! Family friends had a litter of golden retriever puppies, and how could I say no to a golden ball of love, licks and puppy breath? I named him Indiana, after Indiana Jones, and I was truly in love. So was the whole family. He was the perfect dog – friendly, loyal, obedient and, like all golden retrievers, he always seemed to be smiling. Indy, as we called him, died tragically when he was six years old, and my mum and I still haven't recovered. That's the worst thing about having pets – you generally outlive them, and the pain of losing them just breaks your heart. I still have Indy's favourite toy – a soft toy orangutan with its face chewed out. Indy would always chew the faces out of his soft toys, and then my mum would sew flannels in them so they would last.

As I'm sure many people who have lost a dog have done, I got a new puppy shortly after Indy died. Not that this new puppy would replace Indy, but I just felt incomplete without a dog. I do remember feeling like a traitor, though, and wailing, the night before I picked him up, 'I don't want a stupid new puppy, I want Indy back'. This anger soon faded once I had my new ball of fuzz, but of course I'll never forget my precious Indy. The new addition was named Cooper and he was naughty! He would chew my furniture, chew my reticulation and even chew the walls of my house. I had to put up wire sheep fencing to protect my garden. One day when Cooper was about eight months old, I spent three hours planting about $130 worth of new seedlings and plants behind the wire fencing. I gave Cooper chew toys to occupy him while he watched me doing the gardening. I then stupidly decided to return a movie to the DVD store. I was gone for a total of eleven minutes. I came home to see Armageddon on the patio. Cooper had managed to stick his head through the wire fencing, pluck the seedlings from their new home and leave them savaged on his dog bed. Expletives rang out as I saw the carnage, but I could tell as soon as I arrived home that Cooper knew he had been naughty. Luckily, he seemed magically to mature at twenty months and stopped doing anything naughty. His one weakness is reticulation, so I have given up on that!

Apart from that, Cooper really is the perfect dog and everyone adores him, so he wondered why on earth I would bring a kitten home when he was six years old and ruin our tranquil and lovely existence. Boston entered the scene in October 2008 and our lives have never been the same. Boston was a rescue kitten and he ensured that I picked him out from his littermates by constantly coming up to me and gently licking my nose. This loving behaviour was obviously to cover up his true self, since within a few weeks of joining the family he became known as 'Evil Kitty'. In the first year of living with us, Boston left a path of destruction that would normally be attributed to three bull mastiff puppies. He chewed up five mobile phone charger cables, used the furniture as scratching posts, ruined dinners by jumping on the kitchen bench and stealing food, peed in my bedroom on the new carpet, broke a digital phone and answering machine, and destroyed a multitude of other items.

Boston also chewed through my internet modem cable. When I rang various stores trying to find a replacement, the assistant at one store, who found out the voltage it ran on, asked if my cat was still alive. I answered, 'Unfortunately, yes', but of course I didn't mean it. Boston woke me up every morning at 2.00 am and 4.00 am by meowing, biting my face or playing with any number of unknown items shoved under my bed. He would also terrorise Cooper by biting his ankles, jumping on him and stealing his dog kibble. Soon, however, they came to an understanding, and Boston would often curl up to sleep with Cooper on his luxury mattress.

So in a nutshell, since the age of four I have never been without a pet or not been seeking out animals in some way. My mum has an entire photo album that shows my life in pictures with animals, from budgies, cats and sheep to the far more exotic world of otters, monkeys and orangutans when I started work at Perth Zoo. Little did my parents know when they got a guide-dog puppy that it would be the beginning of my animal life!

Cooper and Boston

2

Follow the orange brick road

My first orangutan experience was at Melbourne Zoo when I was fifteen months old. Orangutan twins named Bono and Suma were born at Melbourne Zoo in 1978. Orangutan twins are extremely rare, and in the wild one would usually die, since the mother can't support both infants. The orangutan twins were extremely popular at the zoo, and despite my very young age, Mum said it was love at first sight for me.

It was a long time between Bono and Suma the orangutans and university. University is where my passion for the great apes really took hold, but it certainly didn't happen in first-year uni – I hated it! I studied Environmental Biology, but the majority of first year was a rehash of Year 12 maths and chemistry and then a bunch of other topics I found hideously boring. They included statistics and mycology – the study of fungi, including their use to humans in food (e.g. beer, wine, cheese, edible mushrooms). I couldn't have imagined anything more dull, and the topic held no interest for me. The cheese and wine scenario piqued my interest, but at the time I wondered what this unit was doing in my course when I was on a quest to study animals and become a conservationist.

The few animal-based units in the course kept me hanging on, but at the end of my first year I found myself in my dad's home office having a daddy–daughter deep and meaningful, which included career counselling. My dad has a great business mind, but more importantly he is a fabulous people person, a great listener, and gives advice when appropriate. So he was the perfect person to experience my mini-breakdown as I wailed about how I hated my uni course. I still wanted to work with animals, but I didn't know what to do. Should I quit, travel, change courses, stick it out? I was also terrified, since I thought I had failed my end-of-year exams.

Ironically and fatefully, during my wailing session Mum delivered the mail, which included my university results. I hesitantly opened the envelope and found not only my exam results but a letter of congratulations for being the top biology student of the year. I just burst out laughing and passed the letter on to Dad. By the time he began smirking and shaking his head, Mum was becoming very vocal about being left out, so the letter was passed to her. I was always that annoying student at school who whinged to my friends, 'Oh, I did so badly in that test', and then got a high grade. But I wasn't lying; I would often think I had done badly because I had extremely high standards.

Anyway, that letter was the only reason I decided to finish my university course. During my final years of university I worked closely with a lady called Dr Rosemary Markham, a research fellow at Curtin University who had supervised numerous students undertaking animal behaviour studies, including me. She herself had completed a PhD on orangutans in captivity. She spent years observing the Perth Zoo orangutans and knew them intimately.

I was desperate to study the orangutans for my honours thesis, but Rosemary suggested that I study a different primate species. Due to the highly complex and subtle behaviours of orangutans, she did not think an honours project would provide enough time to complete an accurate study. I grudgingly agreed to study a family group of Sulawesi crested macaques at Perth Zoo. I actually thoroughly enjoyed my time observing this highly social and active primate species, and the project only cemented my desire to work with primates. I obtained a first-class grade for my honours thesis, despite the fact that Rosemary often massacred my initial drafts with red pen and would say to me, 'This is not English literature, Kylie. You need to write in a more scientific manner.' Although I was nearing the end of a science degree, English literature and history had been by far my favourite subjects at high school. Thankfully, I learnt to tone down my Shakespearian flair in time to submit my thesis and finish my university degree on a high note.

January 1999 was a tough month, since I had the after-uni blues – when a fresh graduate says, 'What the hell am I going to do with my life now?' This tends to set in after the Christmas festivities are over and you realise you can no longer live in ignorant bliss while binging on Christmas leftovers, that it's time to enter the real world of full-time employment. I had taken on numerous jobs during my uni degree, and my old schoolfriends still occasionally joke about some of the hideous jobs I had during my studies. The standouts, and not in a good way, were working in a meat factory, of all places, in the lead-up to Christmas, and selling flowers for a vineyard owner outside a cemetery. That job didn't last long, when after selling flowers for more than ten hours on a 42-degree day, my boss proceeded to pay me about $43. He claimed he could only pay me a certain amount based on sales, and I responded that it wasn't my fault if people didn't visit their dead nanna on a 42-degree day and were at the beach instead! Mind you, the ladies at the vineyard did teach me how to do nice bouquets, and I love floristry to this day, so something good came of that job. I also worked in the footwear section of a department store for a few years every Saturday and Thursday night. I would have preferred to work in any other department, since I hate feet, but I needed to earn some money so I stuck with the job for a few years.

Now I did have one 'job' while I was at university that I loved, and that was volunteer work at a native-animal rehabilitation centre called Kanyana. In the late 1960s, a couple named June and Lloyd Butcher purchased 1.2 hectares on the Darling Scarp, east of Perth. As the area became more built up, the human impact on the native wildlife increased. June, a child health nurse, began to take in and care for an assortment of injured animals. The numbers of animals being cared for continued to grow, and in 1986 the Butcher family built a small animal hospital with aviaries attached.

Local people began to volunteer at Kanyana to help care for the animals. Rehabilitated animals would then be released back into the wild. A bilby breeding program commenced in 1994, and the number of people volunteering each week reached 100. I was one of those volunteers. I did a shift once a week that involved caring for a range of orphaned and injured native wildlife, from native parrots to bandicoots. Birds were not my forte, and I still have scars from when some of them pecked me. I was also petrified of the resident emu named R2D2. She had a section of the large property fenced off for her. I would wait until she was up the hill and out of sight and then race in to put her feed in and give her fresh water. On a hot day the hose water would take ages to cool down, and R2D2 would often make her way back down the hill, running and making that weird and creepy drumming noise that emus make. I would pray for the hose water to fill her trough faster so I could make a dash for the gate and escape. And then there was Alison – she was in high school and worked on the same shift as me at Kanyana. She adored R2D2 and would go in with her, get her to sit down and give her scratches and cuddles. She made me look really precious! But I was a mammal girl and loved working with the hairy critters the best. As many mammal keepers will chant, 'If it ain't got hair then we don't care!'

June and Lloyd had two adult daughters, one of whom, Fleur, worked in the primate section at Perth Zoo and would play a vital role in me getting a job there. She had also travelled to Indonesia to work with orangutans. I was in awe. I would pepper Fleur with relentless questions, like a toddler who has just learnt how to talk. Fleur said she would be happy to be a referee for me since I had submitted my resume for work at the zoo while I was doing my honours degree. I was so grateful and excited about the possibilities that lay ahead.

So it was during that dreary month of January 1999 – when I had no job, was bored to tears and stressing about what I would do for the rest of my life – that I received three phone calls on the one day. The first was from my university offering me a PhD scholarship to study Shark Bay mice. I had been encouraged to apply for a PhD due to my high grades, so I applied to keep my options open. The second call was from a five-star resort and casino offering me waitressing work. I had applied for work there as a backup in case none of my immediate animal plans worked out and so I could earn some money while I pursued my dream. The third call was from a guy called Leif Cocks at Perth Zoo, asking if I would come in for an interview about some casual work during summer in the primate section. I said yes to all three and then proceeded to jump around the house screeching like a crazy person because I knew things were about to change!

I don't really remember my interview with Leif. I was extremely nervous because I wanted the work so badly. Leif had been the senior orangutan keeper at Perth Zoo for ten years and had recently begun supervising the primate section. He reminded me in front of the entire zoo staff, when I was acknowledged for working at the zoo for ten years, that when he asked me in that initial job interview what my goal was in life, I answered with, 'To work with gorillas'. Perth Zoo didn't have gorillas and Leif was an orangutan man through and through, but he saw something in me and gave me a short-term contract. I did a little dance of joy after leaving his office. I didn't have a mobile phone back then, so I rushed home to share the good news with my parents. Since it was only casual work at the zoo and I didn't know if it would finish after summer, I also took the casual work at the casino, which was mainly night work. Then I had to deal with the PhD. I felt that I couldn't work at Perth Zoo, do waitressing and do a PhD – something had to give. I turned down the PhD scholarship and followed my heart to the primates at Perth Zoo. I have never regretted it for a second.

3

First impressions don't lie

The primates I worked with initially at Perth Zoo were mainly gibbons, macaques and three chimpanzees. I was so excited to be working with the chimpanzees. They had come from Taronga Zoo in Sydney, and Perth Zoo was caring for them for two years while their future zoo in Japan prepared their exhibit. There was a male named Monty and two females named Sandra and Kike. Each had their own individual personality, as all apes do. Monty was an impressive-looking adult male and was a true gentleman; Sandra was very intelligent but a bit nervous; and Kike was lovely and gentle, and would make night nests for the whole group before they settled down to sleep.

Working with the chimpanzees also gave me my first real insight into positive-reinforcement training. This is when you train an animal to do something by using positive rewards such as verbal praise, a play session or food treats. Chimpanzees, like orangutans, are highly intelligent, and the chimpanzees caught on quickly to the behaviours we wanted them to learn. Behaviours included opening their mouths for teeth inspection, and presentation of various body parts, including the shoulder for future injection when they needed to be transported to Japan. The only behaviours taught were those that would assist with their care, including health checks.

Initially, I mainly trained Sandra. Now Sandra was quite grabby with me at the beginning, so my hands would sometimes end up with scratch marks from her nails when I asked her to place her hands on the mesh. Often I would go straight to my night job at the casino after working at the zoo. This created numerous problems, including the fact that I smelt like chimps and monkeys and had festy scratches on my hands. One night I went to work at the casino with five bandaids on my fingers that I had put on at the zoo. By the end of my kitchen shift I only had four bandaids on. I still don't know to this day if my bandaid fell somewhere innocently on the floor or if it ended up in someone's pasta salad. I soon learnt why you must wear brightly coloured bandaids if you work in a kitchen – so if they end up in the food you can see them!

Although Monty, Sandra and Kike were a well-settled little group and there was hardly any tension, it isn't normally like that in chimpanzee society. Of all the great apes, chimpanzees are the most like humans in their behaviour, and that includes being aggressive at times. Chimpanzees live in multimale–multifemale groups, and related males in a group will form alliances and coalitions to further their position in the hierarchy. Chimpanzees will intimidate rivals by performing aggressive displays that include branch-dragging, loud vocalisations, chasing and attacking.[1] Chimpanzees are the only other species besides humans that exhibit warlike behaviour.

Males in one chimpanzee community have been observed to stalk and kill members of another community until they were all dead.[2] Visitors at the zoo would sometimes say to me, 'Oh, I've seen documentaries about chimpanzees and they are horrible and violent', as if they were a branch below us on the evolutionary tree. My response to this comment was always, 'Yes, but they aren't as violent as humans'. Some people seemed legitimately offended by this statement.

Much as I adored the three chimpanzees at Perth Zoo, there was something that drew me to their gentle and solitary Asian great ape cousins, the orangutans. If I ever finished my afternoon feeds early, I would ask the orangutan keeper if I could visit the 'Orange Kids'. The Orange Kids were ten beautiful Sumatran orangutans, one male and nine females: Hsing Hsing, Puan, Pulang, Punya, Negara, Puspa, Sekara, Puteri, Utama and Temara.

There are two species of orangutan: the Sumatran orangutan (*Pongo abelii*) and the Bornean orangutan (*Pongo pygmaeus*). The Sumatran orangutan is classified as critically endangered according to the IUCN (International Union for Conservation of Nature) Red List, with only about 6,200 remaining in the wild. The Bornean orangutan is classified as endangered, with about 45,000 remaining in the wild. (The IUCN Red List is the world's most comprehensive inventory of the global conservation status of plant and animal species. It uses a set of criteria to evaluate the extinction risk of thousands of species and subspecies.) There are obvious physical differences between the two species of orangutan. Sumatran orangutans have lighter, denser and longer hair; lighter, narrower faces; and more delicate features overall.[3] Unlike their Bornean cousins, Sumatran orangutans, including females, have luxurious beards. Adult males of both species of orangutan develop cheek flanges or cheek pads when they reach maturity.

These are fleshy discs on either side of the face. They don't have a practical function, but they give each male a highly distinctive large-headed appearance. Similarly to the silver back on an adult male gorilla, these cheek flanges show seniority and rank.[4] Most people who work with orangutans would agree that the Sumatran orangutans are the better looking of the two species. The Perth Zoo orangutans are in the supermodel category, since they are particularly good-looking!

As soon as I entered the orangutan area at Perth Zoo, I was grinning from ear to ear. With ten orangutans, it was difficult to choose which one to watch eat, which to play with and which to give my attention to in such a short space of time. A few orangutans particularly stood out, and one of those was Temara. Not because she was overly friendly, sweet or wanted to interact with me, but just because she was…well, Temara!

Born to mother Puteri and father Hsing Hsing on 14 September 1992, Temara was a gorgeous and spirited infant and was soon gracing Perth Zoo certificates and other merchandise. The intellectual capacity of orangutans varies between individuals just as it does with humans. From a very early age, Temara appeared to have inherited the high intellect and quick temper of her father, Hsing Hsing. Puteri took advantage of her daughter's intelligence, teaching Temara, for example, to use the puzzle feeders and cheat with her tiny baby arms. Once Temara got the food out the 'cheater's way', Puteri would take it from her and eat it herself. Temara also inherited her father's temper, so Puteri had her hands full dealing with a highly intelligent and temperamental daughter.

Before I even started working with the orangutans, I heard many a story about young Temara. According to Leif, Temara had a cheeky glint in her eye from birth and proved to be quite a handful for both her mother Puteri and the orangutan keepers.

Hsing Hsing (Photo: Derek Smith)

Temara was just plain naughty, and naughtiness combined with high intelligence is a dangerous combination. When Temara was still an infant, she dropped a large toy – a crate! – on a keeper's head during a contact session in her exhibit.

Experienced orangutan keepers at Perth Zoo are allowed to go into the exhibits with certain orangutans for what we call 'contact sessions'. Orangutan keepers have a very close bond with the orangutans and these sessions are very special. A really bad workday can be quickly turned around by having a play date with an orangutan.

Temara with a collection of her precious toys (Photo: Neil Myers)

Contact sessions are also used to check on the physical condition of an orangutan. This includes their skin and hair, and other small health issues that might arise. Our ability to thoroughly check the animals while visiting them in the exhibit meant that we once found a small hernia on Puteri. Being able to enter the exhibit with the orangutans has other advantages, including being able to remove an item from the exhibit if needed. One hilarious example of this involves an orangutan named Punya and her daughter Negara. Punya was a very shy and conservative orangutan. She liked everything to be just so and was not very accommodating when it came to change and new things. One day Punya was highly distressed and hiding on the top of the climbing structure because seven little ducklings were in her exhibit. She was horrified at this invasion and was hiding under a cardboard box, clutching at Negara in terror.

Occasionally Punya would peer down at the tiny defenceless ducklings and then hide away again under her box. The ducklings could not get out of the exhibit and the mother duck was causing a ruckus nearby as she impatiently called for her babies to follow her. I opened the access door into Punya and Negara's inside area so they could come inside and the keepers could retrieve the ducklings. Punya did not think this was an appropriate course of action, since it would involve her and Negara having to come to the ground and move past the terrifying ducklings. I quickly realised that Punya and Negara could not be convinced to leave their fortress high on the climbing structure, so instead I organised a quick search-and-rescue mission into the exhibit and returned the ducklings to their mother. We couldn't help but see the amusing side of the situation, although I'm sure Punya didn't feel the same way. Being able to enter the exhibit and resolve the situation quickly was an excellent outcome for all involved.

Contact sessions are usually planned in advance and occur about once a fortnight. Orangutans are mostly solitary animals, and just like most people, they don't want their relatives visiting all the time – although the occasional visit from Aunty Sue and Uncle Jack is enjoyed. The orangutans and keepers both enjoy the contact sessions, and each orangutan wants to partake in different activities when the keepers visit. Some want to play, some are focused on what food treats we may have, and some like to be tickled. Many keepers, including me, love to visit an orangutan named Utama. She is Temara's half-sister and really enjoys close physical contact with the keepers. She was hand-raised as an infant and therefore is very friendly with the keepers and certainly enjoys a good tickle session. Temara was quite different from the other orangutans during contact sessions in that she liked to drop things on the keepers' heads and cause trouble. When Temara dropped

Utama enjoying a tickle session

a crate on a keeper's head, it was only the beginning of a long list of 'Guess what Temara did?' stories.

It didn't take me long to realise that this girl had attitude and had outsmarted every orangutan keeper at one time or another. I started working full time with the orangutans in 2000, and it wasn't long before I was on that list. One particular incident I remember was being in the orangutan night dens and hearing a metallic clinking noise coming from one of the exhibits. I went outside and onto the keeper roof where we can see all of the exhibits. As soon as I made my way up onto the roof the clinking noise stopped. All of the orangutans appeared sweet and innocent, including Temara. I went back downstairs and within thirty seconds the clinking started again. I again went onto the roof and – surprise, surprise – all of the orangutans were yet again quiet and angelic. This happened once more, until someone called me on two-way radio and told me that Temara had a padlock off a hanging toy. So this time I went back up onto the roof loaded with food treats and a padlock of my own. I went to Temara's exhibit, showed her my padlock and asked her to give me her padlock in exchange for my bribe. Temara didn't show that she had the padlock until the food treat I held up was good enough – nuts and dried fruit. Once Temara knew that would be her reward, she went and retrieved the padlock from its hiding spot and threw it to me, or rather *at* me. I then gave her the treats and thanked her profusely.

It is imperative that captive orangutans be provided with opportunities to be active, solve problems and undertake natural behaviours. These are important for both their physical and mental health. Every orangutan exhibit at Perth Zoo has various puzzle feeders that increase the foraging time of the orangutans. Some feeders contain a food treat such as nuts that the orangutans have to manipulate through a maze using a stick. Mesh boxes welded to the climbing poles can have whole or frozen fruit placed in them and then locked up. The orangutans have to use their fingers to squeeze the juice of the fruit through the mesh. Many other activities are also provided to the Perth Zoo orangutans to keep them busy.

One day I stupidly left a container of nuts in Puteri and Temara's exhibit when I was placing enrichment in the maze puzzle feeder. I locked up the exhibit without seeing that I had left the container of nuts on the grass, then opened up the night-den slide to let Temara outside. From that viewpoint, when I opened Temara's slide, we both saw the nuts in the exhibit at the same time. Two very different facial expressions then ensued. Mine was a look of sheer horror, knowing that Temara was about to get a free hit of 41,347 calories, while Temara's was one of pure delight as well as a hint of 'Ha, you stuffed up big-time!' Temara hadn't entered the exhibit yet, so I attempted to close the slide and keep her inside while I quickly removed the nuts. An amateur's mistake...Temara made a dash for it and was outside before I had moved the slide even 3 centimetres. She then sat in the exhibit, practically caressing the container of nuts, and ate them one by one, looking at me the whole time. I tried to coax her back inside with a variety of other treats. The irony was, though, that nuts were what I usually bribed Temara with, as they were her favourite food, so there was no way she was giving them up for a less desirable treat. She knew she had won, so I hung my head in shame and sheepishly closed the slide, choosing not to watch her calorie binge any longer.

At Perth Zoo, all of the orangutans come into their night dens in the late afternoon for their last feed of the day. They are kept in overnight during winter, since they do not like the cold winter nights, and of course being from a tropical climate they would not experience such cold weather in Indonesia. In the wild, orangutans settle down to sleep in the early evening at approximately 5.00 pm, so we follow that schedule at the zoo. In the morning, during winter, some of the orangutans will still be fast asleep in their nests when the keepers start work – just as I would still prefer to be in bed on a cold winter's morning. Temara was the worst offender – she would always sleep in and only get up once her breakfast was served. She would often look bleary-eyed and have messed-up hair, so I don't know what she got up to during the night. In the summertime the orangutans have access to their exhibits overnight so they can sleep outside if they wish and start their day with the sun at 5.00 am.

Temara used to be excellent at coming into her den at night. She was taught well by her mother, Puteri, who would enter the den at night in about 0.17 seconds. If there was ever food involved, then Puteri was there, as she loves her food! Temara slept in the same den as Puteri for nine years before she started to rebel and would dawdle with coming into the den. This would greatly disturb Puteri, since the keepers would only feed her once she and Temara were both secured inside the same den. Just like children, animals at a zoo need to have some form of routine at certain times of the day so the keepers can undertake tasks such as cleaning. But just like a rebellious teenager, Temara reached an age when she wanted to do what she wanted when she wanted, and stuff this routine business. Despite Temara's determination to stay outside, it was no match for her mother's desire to eat her dinner. I would say to Puteri, 'Go and get Temara, go on, good girl'. Puteri would then storm back outside and drag Temara into the night den by her ear. I was so grateful for Puteri's discipline, even if it was solely motivated by her rumbling stomach.

Another year went by and it was time for Temara to have her own night den. Puteri and Temara still shared an exhibit during the day but it meant they could have their own space and food during the night. This was following natural orangutan behaviour, as Temara was nearing the age where she would naturally move away from her mother in the wild.

In 2002, Puteri and Temara were moved into a newly constructed orangutan exhibit with three 14-metre-high poles, large resting platforms, numerous smaller flexible poles and many enrichment devices, such as water cannons and feeding puzzles. The exhibit was mainly designed by Leif, with a lot of input from orangutan keepers, including me. The finished exhibit was fabulous. We deliberately chose Puteri and Temara to move in to the new exhibit since Temara was the most active and intelligent orangutan in the colony and would make use of the new infrastructure. The new exhibit was also heavily planted out with a range of plants, herbs and small trees. We knew that these would most likely be destroyed once we let orangutans into the exhibit, but we hoped a few would survive. It is very difficult to have natural-looking exhibits for orangutans. With their size and strength, they quickly destroy any trees and plants in an exhibit that aren't protected with electric fences. Despite the climbing structures being artificial at Perth Zoo, they provide complexity and different travel pathways for the orangutans just as the canopy would in the rainforest.

Well, Temara certainly did make use of her new exhibit equipment. She ascended the new high poles in no time. Puteri, her beautiful mum, was more cautious, and looked up daunted at the new poles for some time before carefully making her way up. Despite Temara using the exhibit to its full potential, she didn't feel the same way about using her new night den and she refused to enter the den in the afternoon. She decided instead to use the lush vegetation in the new exhibit as her own personal Sizzler salad bar. Puteri would enter her night den immediately after the slide was opened. And then there was Temara. She would sit about

10 metres away from the slide, where I could see her, and eat the plants. I would show her an abundance of tasty food from her dinner, including tropical fruits, nuts and eggs, but she just sat there. And ate the plants. I decided to play her game, so I would sit there and eat her food so she could see me. Temara would eat a plant, I would eat some pineapple. Temara would eat another plant, I would eat some carrot. Temara would eat another plant and I would eat an egg. Temara would start nibbling on yet another plant and I would stand up and beg, 'Oh, please, for the love of God just come inside, Temara'. This stand-off continued for weeks as the lush green vegetation in the exhibit became sparser every day. I was suffering from indigestion and weight gain from eating half of Temara's dinner on a daily basis in a futile attempt to coax her inside. Temara finally started to enter her den once she had eaten all of the tasty plants and herbs outside, not due to any of my supposedly fine-tuned ape-whisperer skills.

Temara excelled at many things, including throwing objects with great accuracy and precision. It was a relief that she was in the new exhibit near the back area of the primate building, because it meant she couldn't throw things at the innocent viewing public. This, however, did little to protect the primate keepers, who walked past the back of this exhibit numerous times a day. One day, I saw Antony, a fellow keeper, walking down the driveway wincing and holding his head. I asked him if he was okay, and he said, 'That damn orangutan of yours just threw an iceblock at my head'. Now, when we make orangutan iceblocks, they are not your standard-sized little iceblocks that you eat at the beach. They are made in ice-cream containers with different layers that include fruit and nuts. Each one probably weighs about 1.5 kilograms. After eating half her ice block, Temara thought the other half could be put to better use by pitching it at Antony's head as he walked down to the primate kitchen. As I said, Temara had a very good aim, and she didn't miss. Poor Antony had a shocking headache all day and from then on he would give Temara the evil eye whenever he walked down that driveway. I'm sure Temara chose her target carefully, since Puteri adored Antony and Temara would get very jealous of Puteri's affection for him.

We give the orangutans various toys to play with, but due to the incredible strength of orangutans, they are no ordinary toys. Items such as hard plastic crates, tyres and large boomer balls are given so they can endure the rough treatment. This seemed fine in theory, until one day my dear friend and fellow keeper Petra had a close encounter with one of Temara's toys. Petra and I were chatting on the jinxed primate driveway when, out of nowhere, a racing tyre suddenly landed on Petra's shoulder and made her buckle at the knees. We both looked up to the skies to see Temara perched high up on a pole peering over at us to see if she had hit her target. I apologised profusely on Temara's behalf and gave her a mother-like death stare while checking if Petra was okay.

After this incident, Temara had her tyre confiscated for a short time, but not wanting to miss out on her new game, she found other ways to participate. A week after Petra was hit with the tyre, I was giving a behind-the-scenes tour of the primate area to a small group of zoo visitors. Silly me and my short-term memory – I paused on the primate driveway as I was chatting to the group. One of them had to go to the toilet, which was in our primate kitchen building at the end of the driveway. Coincidently, I was explaining to the group about the intelligence and problem-solving abilities of orangutans. Suddenly there was an almighty bang from the toilet. I wondered if this person had perhaps eaten a hot curry for lunch but no, the cause of the bang was Temara. She had thrown a branch firmly at the toilet door and hit her target directly. Thirty seconds later, the visitor nervously came out of the toilet, not knowing what had happened. Luckily, the group thought it was hilarious and were impressed with Temara's aim. Even with her toys confiscated, Temara found a way to achieve her goals. The branch was from the orangutans' daily feed of fresh-cut foliage. We couldn't exactly confiscate her food!

Any zoo that has open-air great ape exhibits needs to contend with the possibility that their orangutans, gorillas, bonobos or chimpanzees might occasionally throw something out of the exhibit. To prevent this would mean not giving the animals any moveable items to play with, and this isn't fair. The visitors at Perth Zoo love that they can see the orangutans up high on their platforms with the sunshine glistening in their hair and not behind mesh. Due to the number of orangutan exhibits at Perth Zoo, we have the flexibility to move the 'throwers' to exhibits that are further away from the public. This greatly reduces the risk involved with an occasional flying object.

Temara also used to make her presence felt when the keepers visited her and Puteri in their exhibit. Puteri, or Puti as we affectionately call her, is a very friendly orangutan and loves to interact and play with the keepers. She also has a soft spot for the male keepers, and will whimper and play with them the most. Temara didn't approve of her mother cavorting with the keepers and would sometimes try to pull Puteri away from them out of jealousy. Temara would also occasionally nip the keepers if they gave Puteri too much attention. One day Temara kept pulling my hand up towards her mouth to try to nip me. I told her no but she persisted. So to prove that two could play at that game, I proceeded to nip her hand instead. Temara was quite taken aback, but she never tried to nip me again in a contact session. I discovered that orangutan hair is not very tasty.

Temara developed her most famous trait in her younger years. This was digging her thumbnail into keepers' hands. People watching from the window thought it was so sweet when they saw Temara reach out to hold the keeper's hand, and they probably thought it was odd when the keeper would cringe slightly and then slowly remove their hand from Temara's clasp. This was because Temara was not being sweet and gentle and holding the keeper's hand lovingly. Not a chance. Temara was holding the keeper's hand so she could dig her little thumbnail into the delicate flesh of their palm and see if she could make them wince! It was traits like this that just made me love Temara even more.

Young Temara with a cheeky glint in her eye (Photo: Neil Myers)

4

Conservation crusade

I applied for a permanent job at Perth Zoo in late 2000. There were a lot of people vying for the available jobs, so I was extremely nervous and really didn't think I'd get one given I was still quite new. I was at work on the day the curator informed applicants individually of the outcome of the recruitment process. I was one of the last to be called. I had some people telling me that was a good thing, since they told successful applicants last, but other people told me the exact opposite. By the time the curator actually came to speak to me, I was a mass of nerves and perspiration. Thank goodness the first lot of people were right and I was successful. With some other senior primate staff leaving, despite my young age and relative lack of experience with apes, I became the senior orangutan keeper. I was elated and humbled to be given the responsibility of taking a much greater leadership role with the orangutans at the zoo.

In such a short space of time I couldn't imagine ever not having known the Orange Kids, and I spent every spare minute of my time researching both captive and wild orangutans. They were all I would talk about, and I would easily spend more time with the orangutans at Perth Zoo than my own friends and family. While my parents' friends were starting to show photos of their new grandchildren, my mum proudly carried around photos of her 'orangutan grandchildren', as she called them. At least she never had to babysit my kids or change a dirty nappy!

Orangutan babies rarely ever cry or complain, unlike noisy attention-seeking human babies. They are capable of making human-like crying noises, but they really just don't have the need. They are with their mother 24/7, and their every need and want is met. Orangutan mothers are highly attentive, and comfort their infants if they show any signs of distress. Young orangutans stay with their mother for eight to eleven years. Apart from humans, orangutan youngsters have the longest dependency on their mother. Females stay with their mothers for up to eleven years to learn maternal behaviour by watching their younger sibling being raised. The inter-birth interval of the Sumatran orangutan is the longest of any mammal in the world at nine years. This is one reason they are so susceptible to extinction.

My first exposure to an infant orangutan cry was soon after Semeru was born to first-time mother Sekara in 2005. I adore Sekara – she is my favourite orangutan. I know you shouldn't have favourites, but just as it is with humans, you simply click with certain orangutans. Sekara and I clicked from day one and I love the fact that I'm also her favourite keeper. Sekara will often make affectionate hooting noises when I talk to her. If she is ever being cheeky towards another keeper, I only have to say her name and even if she can't see me, she will instantly behave herself and start hooting away. If I go away on holidays, I can't shut her up on my first day back at work!

Sekara gave birth at 1.47 pm on 13 June 2005. I watched the birth from the window of her exhibit. My heart skipped a beat when Semeru made his appearance into the world, because he looked blue and wasn't moving. For a split second I thought he was stillborn, but then he moved his chubby little fingers and I hugged my fellow orangutan keeper Martina so hard that we lost our balance and nearly fell over. Sekara was a wonderful mother from the start, and she showed how much she trusted me by putting Semeru's little fingers through the mesh for me to hold when he was less than one day old. We left Sekara and Semeru to bond overnight in Sekara's night den after the birth. All of the other orangutans were secured inside that night as well due to the cold weather. The orangutans close to Sekara's night den were very nosy and wanted to see the new arrival. It had been ten years since the last orangutan baby had been born at Perth Zoo, so Semeru was extra precious.

When I arrived early the next morning, I was excited and apprehensive about how Sekara and Semeru had gone overnight. I was taken aback when I heard what sounded like a human baby screeching from the orangutan corridor. I entered the corridor and I still remember the scene vividly. Every single orangutan was sitting up in their bed looking dishevelled and sleep-deprived. They were all looking down at Sekara's den as if to say, 'Will you shut that baby up!' Poor Semeru hadn't suckled yet, and he was making it known to everyone within earshot that he was hungry. Poor Sekara looked anxious and tired, as most new mums look if they are having trouble breastfeeding. They both soon got the hang of this suckling business, though, and not a peep was heard from Semeru again. His strong desire for milk was an early

Sekara with her adorable new bundle, Semeru

indicator of what a big appetite he would have and what a huge orangutan he would become.

I knew I was extremely lucky to be working personally with such an amazing species, and I wanted to give something back. Leif, my boss and mentor with a vast knowledge of orangutans, was the founder and president of The Orangutan Project (TOP). The Orangutan Project is a not-for-profit organisation supporting orangutan conservation, rainforest protection and reintroduction of orphaned orangutans into the wild in order to save the species from extinction. TOP is able to distribute funds directly to support conservation projects in the field. The mission of TOP is to promote the survival of the Sumatran and Bornean orangutan species in their natural habitat by undertaking genuine, measurable and effective orangutan conservation.

When Leif asked me to join the TOP board in 2000 I readily accepted. I became a general board member and after a couple of years I became the secretary. In its early stages, TOP raised $30,000–50,000 per annum. In 2005 I became the conservation project manager. Our yearly income had increased to about $400,000, so we could now support more substantial orangutan conservation projects in Indonesia and Malaysia. My role was created to keep track of all of TOP's supported projects, obtain funding proposals and project updates, and make the overseas bank transfers. Being a zookeeper, I was not accustomed to having large amounts of money myself, so I found it quite exhilarating when I sent large sums from TOP's bank account to overseas conservation projects. I'm still in this role on the TOP board and I greatly enjoy it. It keeps my finger on the pulse in the orangutan conservation world, and I'm in regular contact with people working in the field. I also undertake field trips to assess and assist the projects where needed. TOP is now sending more than $1.4 million per annum to orangutan conservation and rehabilitation projects. I think this is an amazing effort for an organisation that started with a small committee meeting once a month in a dimly lit office in Perth.

TOP's board is now national, and includes people from numerous Australian states. Most people involved with TOP are volunteers, and we put a huge amount of time and effort into our communal quest to save our orange cousins. More often than not, I'm on email to other board members on Friday and Saturday nights. TOP has sucked any social life I had into an abyss, but I wouldn't have it any other way. At times I do feel weighed down by the huge, sometimes seemingly insurmountable task of saving the orangutan, but then one of the orangutans at Perth Zoo or a story about an orphaned orangutan baby in an oil palm plantation will inspire me to stop feeling disheartened and get back to work.

From 2001 onwards, the majority of my life has revolved around orangutans, both at the zoo and in my volunteer work for TOP. In 2002, I travelled to Sumatra for the first time with Leif and his wife, Wendy, in a quest to observe orangutans in the wild. We went to Ketambe, a forest area on the edge of the Gunung Leuser National Park in Aceh province. Sumatran orangutans are now only found in the two northern provinces of Aceh and North Sumatra. On one of our jungle treks, our trained orangutan field technician received a radio call that an orangutan had been sighted about a kilometre away. I don't think I had ever seen Leif run before, but he could leg it when a wild orangutan was nearby. Wendy and I followed and we were out of breath by the time we caught up to Leif and the technician.

We finally made it to where the orangutan had been seen and I looked up to see a glimpse of orange hair in the canopy. A wild orangutan! It was a young adult female. We followed her for some time with our necks craned upwards to observe her high in the canopy. I was so thrilled to be in the presence of a wild orangutan that when she urinated I felt quite honoured to be splashed with pee. Everyone thought I was crazy but I didn't care. I had now had physical contact with a wild orangutan – well, sort of. And urine is meant to be sterile anyway.

It was also on this trip that I came face to face with oil palm plantations, which are to orangutans what kryptonite is to Superman. They mean death. Why, you may ask. The single greatest threat facing orangutans is the rapidly growing palm oil industry. Rainforests are being cleared at an alarming rate to make way for thousands of oil palm plantations. (Palm oil is an edible vegetable oil obtained from the fruit of the African oil palm tree,

Elaeis guineensis.) There are vast areas of degraded land in Indonesia that could be used for oil palm plantations, but many companies obtain concessions for plantations in forested areas so they can make further profits by logging and selling the timber first.

Uncontrolled burning is also often used to clear forested land, which results in many orangutans and other animals being burned to death. The few that manage to survive are then left with nowhere to live and no available food. Many orangutans are also killed by oil palm plantation workers, as they are considered pests. Often, orangutans that have lost their forest home will enter the plantations to eat the young oil palm plants because they are starving. They are brutally hunted down and killed in horrific ways, including being burnt alive or hacked to death with

Stuck behind endless trucks laden with logged trees

machetes. If a female orangutan with a baby is killed, then the baby is usually taken and sold illegally as a pet. Orangutans are sometimes captured and chained up at plantation camps where they are usually beaten and only ever thrown the odd scrap of food.

Hundreds of everyday items that people buy contain palm oil, including ice cream, biscuits, chips, crackers, margarine, laundry powders, detergents, toothpaste and cosmetics. Unknowing consumers fill their shopping trolleys with these products and yet another orangutan is slaughtered before the shopping items have even been paid for at the cash register. Palm oil has infiltrated our food industry like a cancer, and it is our closest living relative that will pay the ultimate price: death and looming extinction. Estimates show that if the spread of oil palm plantations into

The blur of continuous oil palm plantations through the car window

forested land does not stop soon, orangutans will be extinct in the wild within ten to twenty years.

Most people are genuinely horrified when they find out about the palm oil industry in Indonesia and Malaysia and its devastating impact on the orangutan, but feel at a loss as to how to help. Product labelling is part of the problem, because products that contain palm oil are only required to list it as 'vegetable oil'. A campaign was launched by Melbourne Zoo in 2010 requesting the Australian Federal Government to initiate compulsory labelling of palm oil in products and to cease imports of palm-oil-based biofuels. Perth Zoo joined this campaign, and more than 130,000 signatures were obtained across the country. The fight still continues to give consumers the right to know if palm oil is in the products they buy.

Despite palm oil being an ingredient in a huge array of consumer products, the current major driving force behind the ever-expanding oil palm industry is its use as a biodiesel. The European Union's aim of reducing greenhouse gas emissions by 20 per cent by 2020, partly by demanding that 10 per cent of vehicles be fuelled by biodiesels, has seen an exponential increase in the number of oil palm plantations in Indonesia and Malaysia. These plantations are the main culprit in the destruction of precious rainforest habitat and yet palm oil, mixed with diesel to produce biofuel, was hailed as a potential saviour of the environment! In simple terms, the benefit of using palm oil as a biofuel was that the oil palm plants produce organic compounds that when burned in engines do not add to overall carbon dioxide levels. The carbon dioxide absorbed by the plant in its lifecycle should balance the amount it gives out when burned.

But this supposed environmental dream has now turned into a nightmare. Huge amounts of carbon dioxide have been released into the atmosphere due to the clearing, draining and burning of forests, including peat-land areas that hold huge amounts of carbon. Much of Central Kalimantan is covered with sodden peat. As the trees in these areas are cut down and the area is drained for future oil palm plantations, it dries out and the stored carbon is released. In Indonesia alone, peat releases 600 million tonnes of carbon per year. On top of this, the forest is often set alight to speed the clearing. These huge forest fires release further carbon dioxide and are responsible for the haze that often blankets much of South-East Asia. Estimates say Indonesia's fires generate 1,400 million tonnes of carbon dioxide each year, now making it the world's third-largest producer of carbon dioxide (after the United States and China), if both factors are taken into account.[5]

Clearing forests causes global warming and land degradation. Environmental groups such as Greenpeace claim that the deforestation caused by the expansion of oil palm plantations and the damage this does to the climate far outweighs any benefits of switching to biofuel.[6]

As well as the devastating impact that oil palm plantations have on the environment, there are many negative social impacts on the local communities. Oil palm is without a doubt a valuable economic crop and is a major source of employment, but the development of new plantations often creates social conflict and an abuse of human rights. Most of the converted area is customary land owned by indigenous people and local communities. These people are often forced to give up their land against their will to make way for new plantations and are not given adequate compensation. Palm oil companies claim that they bring employment opportunities to the area, but often transmigrants move in and take many of the jobs. Wages are also very low for plantation workers, and once the forest has gone, people can no longer use it sustainably to make a living.

The whole community is then reliant on the massive plantations, and this is now causing widespread conflict.

Knowing all I did about the catastrophic impact oil palm plantations have on orangutans and the environment in general, it was with a heavy heart that for much of our road journey through Sumatra I watched as we were stuck behind an endless line of trucks laden with oil palm fruits. As well as the trucks in front and behind our car, we were surrounded by hundreds of kilometres of oil palm plantations on either side of the road. I felt anger and helplessness at the enemy that seemed to be engulfing me: anger because of the greed and short-sightedness of the human race, and helplessness due to the sheer enormity of the problem. Standing out from this, though, was an emerging desire and passion to do even more to save the orangutan from extinction.

5

A new hope

As the conservation work of TOP expanded, we began supporting habitat protection in the Bukit Tigapuluh (BTP) ecosystem in the province of Jambi in Sumatra. Bukit Tigapuluh translates to 'thirty hills'. Sumatra is the sixth-largest island in the world and one of the most resource-rich islands in Indonesia, generating about 70 per cent of the country's export income, and its economy is dominated by petroleum, gas and plantations. The provinces of North Sumatra, Riau, Aceh, South Sumatra and West Sumatra have extensive plantation areas producing palm oil, rubber, cocoa, tobacco, acacia and tea. India and China are the largest buyers of palm oil from Indonesia.

Jambi province is located in Central Sumatra. Sadly, vast areas of forest are being converted to rubber and oil palm plantations at a frenetic pace. Huge plantations cover the eastern lowlands of Jambi province. The timber industry is also huge, with numerous large mills taking in rainforest trees, only to spit them out as woodchips. These are made into paper and pulp products, including office paper and toilet paper. The habitats of some of the world's most endangered species are literally being used to wipe people's arses and then being flushed down the toilet.

The BTP National Park is a 143,223-hectare national park of mostly tropical lowland forest in eastern Sumatra. Most of it lies in Riau province, with a smaller 33,000-hectare pocket in Jambi province. For several endangered species, such as the Sumatran tiger, Sumatran elephant, Asian tapir and many birds, it is their last refuge. Other mammals in the park include clouded leopards, civets, macaques, gibbons and mouse deer.

The Bukit Tigapuluh ecosystem is also home to one of only two reintroduction sites for the critically endangered Sumatran orangutan. Sumatran orangutans have become extinct throughout Sumatra, apart from the two northern provinces of Aceh and North Sumatra. Sumatran orangutans used to live in the BTP ecosystem, but were hunted to extinction in this area more than 100 years ago. With prime forest available and some of the area designated a national park, the BTP ecosystem was chosen to become the first reintroduction site for the Sumatran orangutan. The BTP Sumatran orangutan reintroduction project is a collaborative venture between multiple organisations, including the Frankfurt Zoological Society (FZS), the Sumatran Orangutan Conservation Programme (SOCP) and TOP. Following introductions through TOP, Perth Zoo also came on board as a partner to support the project.

FZS is an international conservation organisation based in Frankfurt, Germany. It is committed to preserving natural habitat and biological diversity in the last remaining wilderness areas on earth, and initiated its groundbreaking orangutan release project

The location of Bukit Tigapuluh National Park

Map based on an image by NordNordWest/Wikipedia. http://creativecommons.org/licenses/by-sa/3.0/de/legalcode

in BTP, with the first release in 2003. FZS supports the national park authorities in protecting the national park, and works with local administrators to reduce pressure on its wildlife by ensuring changes in the land use around it. FZS also encourages community engagement through education and support of sustainable economic development projects for people who live in the forests of the national park.[7]

Sumatran orangutans released at BTP come from the Batu Mbelin Orangutan Quarantine Centre in North Sumatra. Orangutans housed in this centre have either been voluntarily surrendered or, more often, confiscated from their illegal holders. Orangutans can be confiscated from a variety of people and living conditions. Despite the fact that it is illegal to own an orangutan as a pet in Indonesia, this law has rarely been enforced. In fact, it is quite common for government officials and police officers to keep wildlife illegally. Corruption is rife in Indonesia, and people rarely think of animal welfare as they pocket an illegal payment for their latest terrified captive. Sadly, as rampant habitat destruction continues in Indonesia, so too does the opportunity for poachers to capture or kill countless endangered species. With many species, the adults are killed and either eaten or their body parts sold for use in traditional medicines. Youngsters often make the poacher more money when they are sold alive and illegally as a pet.

Inevitably, any orphan orangutan being kept as a pet has probably borne witness to the brutal murder of its mother. A female orangutan is highly protective of her infant and will not surrender her offspring even when her life is in danger. This often results in the infant orangutan seeing its beloved mother killed while it still clings desperately to her hair. Orangutan babies suffer severe psychological trauma after witnessing these events. They are then often bundled into a tiny box or a sack as they are taken to be sold. Many orangutan infants die before being sold due to the emotional and physical trauma they endure.

The supposedly 'lucky' orangutan infants that survive long enough to be sold as a pet are not really lucky at all. Some are kept by families that initially treat them like a member of the family, dressing them in baby clothes and feeding them unsuitable human food. Inevitably, as these infant orangutans grow older and become stronger, they are usually relegated to a cage outside, since they are no longer manageable.

Other orangutans can be kept in horrendous conditions from the moment they are purchased. Countless orangutans held as pets have never been outside their prison-like filthy cage. Never been able to climb. Never been able to see the sky. Some have been chained up for years and bear the physical scars of these insidious chains imprinted in their tender flesh. They are thrown scraps of food and mocked by people. It is a true crime that this magnificent species of the forest can be forced to suffer such a cruel life, so far removed from where they belong and thrive.

More organisations are now active in confiscating illegally held orangutans. In Sumatra, the Sumatran Orangutan Conservation Programme undertakes confiscations and will take the orangutans to their quarantine centre, where they undergo quarantine and full health checks upon arrival. Once the orangutans are in excellent physical health and considered ready for release or pre-release training, they are transported by road to the release site in Jambi. This journey is about 800 kilometres, so it can take more than forty-eight hours, due to traffic, breakdowns and very rough roads.

When orangutans arrive at BTP, they are housed in socialisation cages and undergo intensive pre-release adaptation training. This includes providing the orangutans with various forest foods, including fruits, termite nests, leaves and rotan (rattan) stem. This means orangutans become familiar with these items before being released. Smaller and more manageable orangutans are taken out during the day by technicians to participate in 'forest school'. This time in their natural habitat allows the young orangutans to learn vital forest skills such as climbing, foraging and nest building. Preparing orangutans for release back into the wild is a very labour-intensive process. Recently, numerous documentaries have been made about rehabilitating orangutans. Each animal is closely monitored after release, and detailed observation records are kept. The first orangutans were released at BTP in 2003, and more than 150 have since returned to their true jungle home.

Pre-release cages

In order to protect these newly released orangutans and the forest habitat surrounding the release site, Wildlife Protection Units (WPUs) were established in 2004 and funded by TOP. The main objectives of the WPUs are to stop and prevent illegal logging in the BTP area, to actively assist with the reintroduction and translocation of orangutans in BTP, to collect wildlife data in the BTP ecosystem, and to educate local communities about habitat protection. Members of the WPUs are trained in land navigation and orientation, basic life support and first aid, equipment maintenance, basic wildlife crime investigation, patrol management and leadership skills. The WPUs are especially important in trying to protect the buffer zone of the BTP National Park, which is prime habitat for the critically endangered Sumatran elephant and Sumatran tiger.

Wildlife Protection Units in training

Leif visited this reintroduction site in 2005 and met the project director, Dr Peter Pratje, a biologist from Germany. Peter has dedicated years of his life to establishing and overseeing this vital reintroduction project. He conducted a thorough vegetation survey of the area before the release site was established, to ensure it had enough suitable fruit trees for released orangutans. Most of his focus is now on securing areas of land within the BTP ecosystem to ensure it does not meet the same fate as so much other forest in Indonesia. During Leif's visit, Peter told him about a young male orangutan named Tatok who was in the socialisation cages and appeared to have psychological problems. Tatok had most likely suffered trauma at the hands of his owner

Peter Pratje with one of his charges (Photo: Peter Pratje)

when he became an unwilling pet for someone's amusement. He had also almost certainly seen his own mother murdered before he was snatched as an infant or juvenile and taken from her dead body.

All of the young orangutans at rehabilitation centres in Sumatra and Borneo have lost their mothers and have usually experienced severe psychological trauma from being witness to their own mother's death. Some of these infants have seen heart-breaking atrocities. Young orangutans sometimes have physical scars themselves as a testament to how their mother was slaughtered. This may be burns on their small and frail body from when their mother was burnt alive or a missing hand or foot that was still desperately grasping its mother's hair as she was brutally killed by a machete-wielding oil palm worker. Emotional trauma also comes with such an event, and this has a huge impact on how a young orangutan might cope with the rehabilitation process and whether it is successful when released back into the forest.

When Leif observed Tatok, he saw behaviours such as rocking from side to side, a vacant expression and fear of the technicians who look after the caged orangutans. He was also highly introverted. Leif suggested to Peter that Tatok might benefit from positive-reinforcement training and suggested that I could be an excellent candidate to help with his rehabilitation. When Leif spoke to me about this upon his return, I was extremely keen to visit the release site and do my best to give Tatok a second chance at returning to the forest from which he was taken.

Positive-reinforcement training works by using praise and rewards, rather than punishment, to teach an animal particular behaviours. It is very common in dog training. The best success with positive-reinforcement training in dogs is achieved by finding out what motivates the dog and then using that as a reward. The reward could be a food treat, verbal praise, a good belly rub or a quick game of fetch with their favourite toy. First, specific cue words or visual signals, such as saying 'Sit' or 'Stay', must be used to prompt the dog to undertake the behaviour. Timing is very important, and the trainer must reward the dog immediately after they respond correctly to the cue.

When a dog is learning a new cue, rewards should be given every time the behaviour is performed correctly, to reinforce the action. But once the dog has learnt the cue and responds to it consistently when asked to, rewards don't need to be given every time. Verbal praise such as 'Yes' or 'Good boy/girl' can be used to reinforce the behaviour. Sometimes a clicker or whistle is used as a 'bridge' to reinforce the correct behaviour instead of verbal praise. Timing is also crucial when using these items, and the bridge must be given at the exact moment the correct behaviour is undertaken. By only giving intermittent rewards such as food treats or a scratch, the session is kept interesting, as the dog doesn't know when it will receive a reward.

Some of the orangutans at Perth Zoo undertake short positive-reinforcement training sessions to assist with their care and to encourage mental activity and learning. Most trainers at the zoo use a whistle as a bridge, as it leaves both hands free. There is an art to learning how to hold the training whistle in your mouth while still giving clear verbal cues. One must also be adept at blowing the whistle at exactly the right time and not constantly blowing into the whistle while giving verbal cues to the orangutan, or it will create utter confusion. It also took some time for me to learn not to choke on my whistle. All orangutan keepers at Perth Zoo are taught how to use positive-reinforcement training because Hsing Hsing, Temara's father, has diabetes, which he developed as a result of his diet at his previous zoo. He requires daily insulin injections and regular finger-prick blood samples to test his blood glucose levels. All of this is achieved through short positive-reinforcement training sessions.

Hsing Hsing is excellent with his training sessions and is usually very obliging, despite us asking him to do some unpleasant but highly necessary things! He is rewarded with his favourite food treats, such as nuts and natural yoghurt, as well as verbal praise. For his insulin injection we ask for 'Shoulder' and tap our shoulder with the opposite hand. Hsing will then press his shoulder up against the mesh and allow us to inject him with insulin. For the blood samples we ask Hsing to put his hand through a special training bar. We tap on the bar and say, 'Hand'. We then use a small needle to prick his finger and obtain a small drop of blood. You'd think getting a small drop of blood from a 100-kilogram orangutan would be easy, but sometimes it really is like getting blood out of a stone.

Hsing usually sits there patiently with his hand through the special training bar while his keeper squeezes like mad to try to get enough blood for a blood glucose reading so we know how much insulin to give him. I did say usually. Sometimes Hsing, annoyed by his pesky keeper stabbing his finger and squeezing it for a measly drop of blood, will take the odd swipe at a keeper, including me. The training bar is designed so he can't grab a keeper, but it doesn't stop him having a go every now and then and scaring the wits out of the poor keeper. As a new keeper, it can be very daunting to try to get blood from Hsing after being given the warning spiel from a senior orangutan keeper. As an old hand at this, I just raise my eyebrows at Hsing if he has a swipe at me and ask for his hand again, which he then meekly puts back through the training bar. Hsing is mostly bluffing, so if you stand your ground like a firm parent he will generally cooperate.

Hsing is a very good reminder to new and experienced keepers alike that orangutans are extremely strong and need to be treated with the utmost respect. Orangutans are mostly very gentle, but just like humans they can lash out at times. As a human and therefore a member of the weaker species by far, you do not want to be on the receiving end of an orangutan temper tantrum. Hsing knows many other behaviours, including opening his mouth so we can check his teeth and gums; presenting different body parts including hands, feet and head; and also moving onto a large set of scales so we can monitor his weight.

Numerous other orangutans at Perth Zoo also participate in positive-reinforcement training sessions. All of the behaviours we teach the orangutans are to assist with important husbandry requirements such as weighing, checking various body parts and brushing teeth. No silly tricks are taught.

Another adult male at Perth Zoo is Dinar, and I love doing training sessions with him. Dinar arrived at Perth Zoo in 2004 from Toronto Zoo in Canada. Poor Dinar spent more than thirty-six hours in a specially made transport crate to travel almost 20,000 kilometres to his new home. I clearly remember going to the airport to pick him up. It's not often that an orangutan arrives at Perth Airport, and Dinar was certainly the centre of attention. Airport staff were of course very curious about this new arrival, and were chatting quite loudly and excitedly near Dinar's crate. I heard someone say, 'God, it stinks', and I became instantly defensive. I rushed over to the crate and said, 'You'd stink too if you'd been stuck in a crate for nearly two days'. They looked a bit sheepish after having been told off by a fiery 155-centimetre Italian Australian girl (me) defending her new arrival.

I approached the crate quietly and peered in. It was hard to see in properly but I could make out a massive head and two brown eyes peering out nervously at me. I introduced myself and said his name numerous times to reassure him that everything was okay. I realised I probably should have practised a Canadian accent to make him feel more at home, but I'm terrible at accents – whatever accent I attempt I end up sounding Indian and making a joke about pappadums. I offered Dinar a large drink of hydrolyte through a small meshed section of the crate and he drank it in 2.4 seconds flat. And with that we were instant friends. I bonded with Dinar very quickly and I absolutely adore him. Keepers laugh at me all the time about my soft spot for Dinar the gentle giant. I only have to see a photo of him on my screen saver and I go all mushy. Dinar is 107 kilograms and a big sook. He is very gentle and so obliging when it comes to moving to a different exhibit, being weighed or generally doing anything we ask of him.

Dinar and Hsing Hsing are polar opposites when it comes to how they interact with female orangutans. Hsing is very dominating and aggressive and will forcibly mate with females at times when they are housed together. It is often impossible for keepers to separate Hsing from the female for feeding when they are housed together. Hsing is highly possessive of certain female orangutans and he will sit under the slide so the keeper cannot separate him from the female. This can be very frustrating, since Hsing is a fussy eater and can take longer than a stubborn toddler to eat his dinner! More often than not, while Hsing is pondering which morsel of food to nibble on, his female housemate will have sauntered over and stuffed half his dinner in her mouth without Hsing even noticing. Even more frustrating than that is when Hsing actually hands the female the items of food he doesn't like from his dinner, such as cauliflower, broccoli, cabbage or any other particularly healthy item. Orangutan keepers will pull their hair out, since it is vital, due to his diabetes, that Hsing receive his full ration of food. There are times when no amount of encouragement or positive reinforcement training will drag Hsing away from his new love interest.

Despite Dinar's huge size, he is very placid with the females, to the point where some keepers have questioned his sexual preferences. On more than one occasion a female orangutan has tried to solicit the attention of Dinar only to have him turn away from them and look at a wall or put a hessian sack over his head so he can't see them. Perhaps, since Dinar knows the ladies will come to him, he does not need to make any effort. Orangutan keepers may have encouraged Dinar to think he doesn't need to make an effort due to the affectionate nickname I bestowed upon him and most keepers now use – Handsome.

Dinar loves his food and therefore he is highly motivated to participate in positive-reinforcement training, since it means his favourite treats are on offer. Dinar's main keeper from Toronto Zoo, Karyn, came over with him and stayed for a week to help settle him in. Dinar had already been taught numerous behaviours at Toronto Zoo, including presenting different body parts and opening his mouth wide for inspection. Dinar's willingness to partake in training proved to be highly valuable upon his arrival at Perth Zoo, because he had a small wound on his neck from the long journey to Perth. Dinar obligingly let Karyn inspect and treat this wound, which was wonderful. I watched Karyn train Dinar intently so I could then follow on with these sessions. As time went by I proceeded to teach Dinar some new behaviours, including having his teeth cleaned. Great apes often experience teeth problems in captivity, so oral hygiene and dental checks are important. Dinar was already very good at opening his mouth for inspection, so I built on this behaviour. I introduced a toothbrush dipped in water and desensitised him to letting me brush his teeth lightly with the toothbrush. He

Handsome Dinar at Perth Zoo in 2008

didn't seem to mind at all, so I progressed to using toothpaste very quickly. The vets approved a children's toothpaste that was safe if swallowed.

During the next two weeks, Dinar tried to eat about twelve toothbrushes because he loved the taste of the toothpaste so much. He would clamp down on the toothbrush while I was cleaning his teeth and proceed to suck every skerrick of toothpaste off the toothbrush. Rather than react to this and beg for the toothbrush back, I would just wait patiently and then ask Dinar to return the toothbrush. Sometimes I got the toothbrush back in one piece and other times I would receive bits of the toothbrush over a few minutes. I would verbally praise him for returning the toothbrush but I did not give him a food reward or this would encourage him to steal it more often. To prevent further toothbrush thievery, I began to brush Dinar's teeth for only a couple of seconds and then give lots of praise and rewards if he didn't steal the toothbrush. I slowly extended this time so I can now brush Dinar's teeth, including his back molars, for up to thirty seconds. Dinar now knows he still gets the toothpaste flavour but also lots of other treats if he doesn't eat the actual toothbrush.

Another fabulous story involving positive-reinforcement training is when I discovered that Sekara was pregnant. I took some holiday leave in October 2004 for a couple of weeks. At that time, Sekara was in with Dinar for breeding. It was the first time she had been in with a male and, after being very nervous of Dinar at first, she soon discovered he was very gentle and she became besotted with him. Sekara is a very active and alert orangutan, but when I came back from holidays I noticed immediately that she seemed very subdued and sooky. She was also not very interested in her food. My first thought was that she was pregnant.

I excitedly ran up to the Veterinary Department and obtained a pregnancy test. Orangutans are 97 per cent genetically similar to humans, so they can be put on the human female contraceptive pill and tested for pregnancy with human pregnancy test kits. I waited for Sekara to urinate in her night den and then I secured her in the outside exhibit so I could access her pee. My hands were nearly shaking as I collected her urine with a syringe and did the pregnancy test. It was the first ever pregnancy test I had done – and it was for an orangutan! I waited excitedly but the test came up negative. I didn't believe it. I told some of the other keepers that Sekara was acting strangely but the pregnancy test had come up negative. They all told me not to worry and that it would happen soon. I said quite simply to them, 'I don't believe the test. She's pregnant'.

I went back into the corridor and called Sekara back inside to do a training session with her. I had taught Sekara to present her nipples and genital area in preparation for a possible pregnancy. When I asked her to present her genital area I nearly fell over backwards since there was obvious pink swelling. When a female orangutan is pregnant, her genital area becomes pink and swollen. I gave her lots of praise and food treats and then bounced my way out of the corridor, hugging myself in delight.

As it turned out, only some brands of human pregnancy test kits show a positive result for an orangutan pregnancy. I spoke to Leif about it and he couldn't remember the name of the test they used previously when the orangutans were breeding. Therefore, on my next days off from work, I found myself in a pharmacy with my mum while we were out shopping, looking at all the different pregnancy tests. My poor mum seemed quite embarrassed and wandered off to look at the various brands of sunscreen – what mother wants to be looking at pregnancy tests with her unmarried, single daughter? I bought a few different pregnancy tests and took them to the zoo the next day. My suspicion was proven correct, as one of the pregnancy tests came up positive immediately. I was then able to share the excitement with the other primate keepers, although just as for an expectant human female, we kept the news quiet until Sekara had made it safely through the first trimester. When the pregnancy was announced, Sekara and I made our debut on the front page of the state's newspaper on Valentine's Day. How exciting!

In June 2005, Sekara gave birth to the beautiful Semeru, who was named after a volcano in Indonesia. In October I had to say goodbye to the precious bundle of fuzz for six weeks as I headed off to Sumatra to try to help the young male orangutan Tatok. Unlike Semeru, Tatok had not had the comfort and guidance from his mother that every young orangutan needs to be able to succeed on their own in the jungle. I was hoping I might be able to help Tatok develop some skills to enable him to be released into the forest and return to the life that had been cruelly stolen from him.

6

All you need is love

My mission to help young Tatok began at a tiny airport in Jambi, Sumatra, after flying in from Jakarta. The airport's luggage travelator went for 5 metres and then just ended, so if you didn't get your bag in time it would fall onto the floor. I think the reason they do this is so people pay for one of the thirty-seven porters jumping around madly to actually locate your bag and grab it before it hits the floor. I had no idea where my wallet was even if I had wanted to pay someone, so I collected my trusty backpack by myself. I was the only white person there and obviously I was quite a spectacle, since I was surrounded by people gawking at me. Peter Pratje picked me up but I soon found out he would not be coming with me to the release site, which was ten to thirty-six hours' drive away depending on how many times the vehicle broke down or how bad the muddy track was that led to the release site.

I was bundled into an old red Toyota 4WD jeep with the Indonesian equivalent of Mr Miyagi from the *Karate Kid* movies. He was about sixty, short and with a manic side to him. He would drive like a crazy person on the main road going through town, playing chicken with oncoming traffic. When he saw me grip the seat and grimace he would throw his head back and laugh. If I thought the roads in the city were crazy, I hadn't seen anything yet. The 30 kilometres of dirt road leading to the release site would easily beat any 4WD tracks in Australia – or the world, for that matter. It took eight hours to travel those 30 kilometres, so that is an average of 3.75 kilometres per hour – not exactly fast! This was because for much of the journey, the jeep was either broken down, bogged in mud, on a 45-degree angle in a ditch or overheated with the bonnet up and radiator steaming. The road was just troughs of mud in parts, but the old 1980s-model Toyota 4WD fought gallantly and got us there in the end. I'm sure they could film a very entertaining *Top Gear* special just on that crazy track!

It was very daunting arriving at the release site. I had thought Peter would come down with me but there I was, alone in a strange country. I barely spoke any of the language, and the only other women there were two cooks – a lady and her thirteen-year-old daughter. And no one spoke English. Suddenly my thirty-nine days at this release site seemed like an eternity – it is, after all, exactly the amount of time contestants spend on the reality show *Survivor*. I'm a bit of *Survivor* junkie, along with my friend Petra. We will text each other during the show in horror at some people's lies and deception. We laugh when people have breakdowns on Day 4, claiming that they can't possibly go on because it's so difficult and challenging. I generally yell at the TV, 'Oh, suck it up, it's only thirty-nine days, for crying out loud', while stuffing popcorn into my mouth. I now knew, though, that if a camera was put in front of my face at that moment at the orangutan release site, I would probably blurt out, 'I just can't do this!' I asked myself, 'What was I thinking? Thirty-nine days is such a long time. I want to be on my couch, watching TV and drinking a nice glass of wine'.

I was taken down to the veterinary clinic where I would be sleeping. I had a very basic room with a rickety bookshelf and a small wooden bed. The mosquito net above the bed had more holes in it than a block of Jarlsberg cheese. There was an outside *mandi* room (bathroom) with a squat toilet. A *mandi* involves washing yourself by using a plastic jug to pour cold water from a big bucket onto yourself. The idea of standing there pouring cold water over myself seemed quite unappealing, but having a *mandi* very quickly became one of my favourite things to do after spending hours in the humid and sticky rainforest.

I didn't really know what to do with myself, so I wandered around a bit and took a few photos of the release site. I had a new digital camera, and I wanted to have a practice before I used it to take photos of the orangutans. The release station consisted of the vet clinic, an orangutan food storeroom and preparation area, small huts for the employees to live in, a tiny kitchen and seating area for meals, and the orangutan cages. The kitchen and huts were at the entry area to the station. A small bridge over a river had to be crossed to get to the path that led to the orangutan cages, food store and vet clinic.

I headed up to the small kitchen at about 6.00 pm for some dinner, which consisted of rice, vegetables and chilli – lots of chilli! And I really wasn't used to burning-hot Indonesian chilli. I tried to stop my eyes watering and nose dripping while everyone stared at me eating, but to no avail. I stayed up at the kitchen for about thirty minutes and tried as best I could to communicate with some of the boys up there. Well, they were probably men, but Indonesian men in their twenties tend to look like they are about twelve years old, so it's hard not to call them boys. They also manage to make a normal size-10 white girl like me feel like I'm hugely overweight, since they generally weigh less than 50 kilograms! My communication efforts resulted in me waving my hands around a lot, as people of Italian descent tend to do, and the Indonesian boys all laughing at me.

I went back to the vet clinic and decided to read in my room for a while. I was exhausted from the day's travelling, a dehydration headache had set in and I didn't have the energy to be sociable, especially when that meant being laughed at. The release site only had power for about three hours a night – from 6.00 to 9.00 pm, or earlier if that was when the last person went to bed. I found this out on about my third night, when I was in the outside loo and suddenly the lights went out. I've never been anywhere as black as that night. Of course, it was when I was squatting over the toilet with my pants around my ankles that the lights went out. Of course, I had left my head torch inside the vet clinic. I cursed while I pulled my pants back up and tried not to fall into the squat toilet. I was never to make that mistake again. I had to fumble my way back inside and into my room, nearly ripping the mosquito net as I stubbed my toe on the bed frame and stumbled onto the bed while swearing.

As I was reading my book on that first night, anxious about what my first morning at the release site would bring, I heard a knock on the main door of the vet clinic. I was quite surprised, but my first and ridiculously hopeful thought was, 'Oh, Peter has come down to the site after all and has come to let me know. I'm saved!' I was wrong. I left my room and padded softly across the main front room of the vet clinic and opened the door. Standing there was one of the Indonesian technicians who worked at the site. I remembered seeing him at dinner. I didn't have a clue what he wanted, but he seemed to be gesturing that he wanted to come inside. I thought he might need something from the vet clinic, so I pointed to the storage cupboards but he shook his head. He then pointed to some chairs in the corner of the room and it struck me that he wanted to come in for a chat…or something. Considering it was 9.00 pm, he didn't speak English and I didn't speak Indonesian, I didn't really see what kind of chat we were capable of having. I then started to panic. I was the only white girl at an orangutan release site in the middle of the jungle, it was 9.00 pm and I had a strange man wanting to come into my room. The overreactive part of my brain was thinking, 'Oh my God, I'm going to get assaulted'. The small amount of Indonesian I knew just left my brain and I couldn't think of anything to say to encourage him to leave. I suddenly remembered the word for sleep, which is *tidur*, so I started saying that and putting my head on my folded hands to indicate that I was tired and wanted to go to sleep. Then I panicked that I might be indicating I wanted to sleep with him, so as a last resort I did a nervous Japanese-style bow and closed the door on him. I locked the door and ran back to my room. I dived under the mosquito net and lay there repeating to myself, 'Only thirty-nine days to go, only thirty-nine days to go'.

I don't really remember sleeping that first night, but I must have finally fallen asleep, since I woke up at about 5.00 am to the sound of gibbons calling and insects trilling. I went up and had breakfast, which was more rice, and took solace in the fact that I might lose some weight while living out here for six weeks. I went up to the large orangutan socialisation cage at 9.00 am, as I had arranged to meet the head technician. The whole cage complex itself is built on stilts about 2.5 metres above a concrete pad. This is so food scraps and orangutan waste fall between the bars and onto the concrete to help with hygiene. The cages are cleaned twice a day. The large cage complex is divided into four different compartments. Small lockable doors can be opened between the cage compartments so the orangutans can be moved around to join other groups or be isolated. The cages are about 8 metres high and have flexible rubber ropes in them so the orangutans can climb, exercise and play in the cages. To get up to the cages you have to either walk up an extremely old and half-rotten staircase with massive gaps between the wooden slats, or drag yourself up a slippery wooden ramp. There is a large platform that you can then stand on to observe and feed the orangutans.

Once we were up on the platform, the technician showed me which orangutan was Tatok. He was in the largest cage compartment with five other young orangutans. In actual fact, I didn't need to be shown which one was Tatok. I could tell which one he was immediately just by the description Leif had given me. Physically, he was a gorgeous orangutan; he had a long beautiful coat and a lovely face, with his hair parted down the middle on his head. His forehead was quite prominent, and he had sad, distant eyes. But it was his behaviour that gave away his identity. He was sitting quietly by himself in the corner of the cage while the other young orangutans played and wrestled with each other. When the other technicians came up to clean the cage, they spoke very loudly to each other and used a portable generator to pump water for cleaning. This disturbance greatly agitated Tatok, and he began rocking from side to side. Sadly, some of the technicians thought this was funny and would laugh at him. He really was a lost little soul, and I started to worry that maybe he had endured too much in his short life to be able to succeed in the wild, and that six weeks wouldn't be enough time for me to help him.

I decided the best way for me to help Tatok was to go back to the scientific techniques I'd used to study animal behaviour and observe him intently for three days, to assess his behaviour and what instigated his stereotypical rocking behaviour. During the day, all of the young orangutans in Tatok's cage went out for forest school so Tatok was by his lonesome for six hours. Now orangutans are naturally solitary animals, but at this age Tatok would still have been with his mother in the forest, so he cut a very lonely figure sitting there by himself in the big cage. Tatok had been taken out to forest school in the past but would often come to the ground and rock or just sit in a tree and not forage for food or undertake other natural orangutan behaviours. The orangutans that did not attend forest school were fed multiple times during the day. Tatok had a negative reaction to the loud technicians when they fed the orangutans in the cages. As the technicians fed the other orangutans first and spoke loudly, Tatok would become agitated and sometimes begin to rock from side to side. Some technicians would laugh at him and then give him the food. What the technicians didn't realise was that they were reinforcing Tatok's negative behaviour when they fed him while he was rocking.

Many people make the same mistake with their own pets – they will offer them a treat to distract them from their bad behaviour, such as a dog barking. The animal then realises that if they undertake the bad behaviour in the first place, they will get a treat when they stop. Another mistake people can make is to give their dog negative attention when the dog does something wrong, such as jumping up on people. They will tell the dog off or push it down when the correct thing to do is turn away from the dog and ignore this behaviour. The dog is undertaking this behaviour to get the owner's attention, so the best way to stop it is to remove your attention altogether. The dog will soon get the idea, and should then be rewarded for undertaking desirable behaviours, such as sitting or lying quietly on their bed.

As well as observing Tatok, I began to start some positive-reinforcement training with him. He seemed to take an immediate shine to me, which was a very positive thing if I was going to have any sort of a breakthrough with him. I spoke to him softly and gently, and he never rocked when it was just us. He even let me touch him and give him the odd little tickle or scratch. I started teaching him very simple behaviours, and he seemed quite interested in our short sessions. I would get him to 'target' with his hands, so if I put my right hand up on the mesh he would touch it with his left hand. I also got him to 'move station' (which was simply calling him over to a different spot in the cage) and when he sat in front of me he was rewarded. I then started trying to teach him to open his mouth by cupping water in my hand and splashing small drops in his mouth.

Some people would ask, why bother trying to teach an orangutan such things if you want them to be able to live in the forest? These behaviours appear irrelevant. Yes, some of the behaviours themselves may not relate to any skill required by an orangutan to live in the jungle, but it is all about mental stimulation. Orangutans are highly intelligent, and when they live in the jungle they are constantly stimulated physically and mentally as they travel around and forage for food. Orangutans are the heaviest mammals to live in trees, and they have to navigate high in the canopy and find pathways that will support their weight. They test the strength and safety of small branches and vines before crossing into another tree. Mothers will make a bridge from one branch to another if her youngster's arm span is too small to make the crossing. Orangutans need to have a mental map of the forest and know which areas have fruiting trees at certain times of the year. They use tools to utilise various food sources such as termites and honey, and can problem-solve. This means that if orangutans are stuck in a cage with nothing to do, they become easily bored and can develop stereotypical behaviours. Behavioural enrichment and positive-reinforcement training sessions can help alleviate this boredom while also promoting mental stimulation and learning. If an orangutan is mentally healthy and capable of learning, it has a much greater chance of surviving when released into the wild.

Behavioural enrichment is a vital part of captive animal care. It aims to increase the quality of life of the animal by creating a stimulating environment for physical and psychological wellbeing. Ideally, behavioural enrichment should increase the opportunity for species-specific behaviour, such as foraging, tool use, digging and so on; reduce stress levels and stereotypical behaviours such as rocking or pacing; and increase the activity levels of the animal. Keepers give the orangutans at Perth Zoo a plethora of behavioural enrichment, and we love thinking of new ways to keep our charges busy. Examples of enrichment include food puzzles and mazes, scatter feeds, frozen fruit, large toys, iceblocks, hoist baskets and dip tubes, where the orangutans need to use sticks to retrieve a treat such as yoghurt or mashed fruit from inside a metal pipe. Promoting natural behaviours is especially important for orangutans at rehabilitation centres. They can then directly transfer these skills to their forest environment, making the adaptation process easier. Examples of these include nest building, tool use and specific techniques to obtain difficult natural food sources.

I gave Tatok extra enrichment, including large leaves to play with and sticks so he could 'fish' for food treats that I put out of his normal arm reach outside the cage. Tatok caught on quickly as to how to reach the food treats with his fishing sticks, and would play with the other items I gave him. He would also use the natural forest enrichment that the technicians gave the orangutans during the day, including termite nests and a spiky plant called rotan that has a nutritious inner stem. To access the inside edible part of the rotan, the orangutans have to spend a lot of time manipulating it and shredding the outside prickles off with their hands and teeth. I was relieved to see that Tatok had the ability and desire to participate in these activities, and it gave me hope that maybe I could develop these skills further to help him adapt to life in the forest.

On the third day at the release site, disaster struck in the form of an adult female orangutan named Santi. I wasn't aware that

Tatok playing under a giant leaf

Santi even existed, but I later found out that she had been released the previous year. She was competent in the forest, but she had recently returned to the release site to steal food from the cages at feeding time. She had a young infant with her. I had been playing with Tatok at the cage while his cage mates were out at forest school. I decided to collect some large leaves for Tatok to play with. I left my backpack on the platform out of Tatok's reach and tentatively made my way down the rickety staircase. I only ventured about 30 metres away from the cage area, but as I turned around to go back to the cage, I gasped with horror at what had occurred in that short thirty seconds. At first I thought Tatok or one of the other orangutans had escaped, because an orangutan was climbing on the outside of the cage. I then saw the orangutan was carrying a baby and realised it was an adult female and not an orangutan from the cage. I didn't know who this orangutan was, just that she had my backpack, which contained my new digital camera, and that it was increasing in altitude by the second as she climbed to the roof of the cage complex.

I ascended the stairs like a gazelle in my quest to retrieve my backpack. I knew in my head it was going to be a futile exercise, since once an orangutan has a prize like that you will be hard pressed to get them to part with it. Not only did this backpack have my camera, it contained my extra-strength mosquito repellent, raincoat, sunglasses and my lunch of rice, vegetables and chilli. I started to talk gently and calmly to Santi in order to somehow get my backpack safe in my arms. She looked at me nonchalantly and kept climbing. The cage was about 12 metres high. It had horizontal bars every 60 centimetres, so I grabbed on and started climbing after her. As I neared the top of the cage, Santi sat down on the cage roof and opened my backpack. The first thing she took out was my raincoat. That didn't hold much interest for her so she put it to one side. Then out came my lunch. 'Yes', I thought, 'open the lunch and eat that'. She also put that to one side. 'Damn', I thought. Then she took out my Rid aerosol mosquito repellent. She bit into the bottle and my malaria protection vapourised in one quick 'poof' into her face. Santi was not impressed with that.

My heart sank as Santi pulled out her next prize: my precious new camera – the $645 camera that I hadn't even used until I arrived in Sumatra. Now I knew from my own experience with orangutans, as well as from other people's accounts, that there is no point fighting over anything with them. The orangutan will end up with the disputed item and you'll probably end up injured and sulking. I contemplated trying to get the lunchbox so I could open it and show her my lunch. Maybe she would prefer rice to the art of digital photography. As I slowly inched my way closer to the lunchbox, a loud scream from behind us made Santi and me jump. Puji, one of the technicians, was coming down the path to feed the orangutans in the cage. He had seen me on the roof of the cage with Santi and he started screaming at Santi, and perhaps me, to get off the cage. I could not stop the scene that then unfolded before me. Santi knew she was in trouble, so as if to make a peace offering to the hollering technician below, she threw my camera down towards him. My camera plummeted the 12 metres to the cold stone concrete pad on which the cage was built. I heard a thud but I didn't know if it was my camera hitting the concrete or my heart cementing itself at the bottom of my chest cavity. Santi then grabbed my now mostly empty backpack and scaled the nearest tree to escape the angry technician.

I climbed back down the cage and onto the platform and then made my way down to the concrete pad to retrieve my camera. I couldn't bring myself to look at it. I then had to wait another forty minutes for Santi to slowly drop the rest of my possessions to the ground as she lost interest in them. Once I had collected them all up, I slowly shuffled my way back down the path and to the solace of the vet clinic. I took my camera out of its case and it was literally bent in half. And then I bawled. I was so upset and angry that I just cried and cried. I also kicked the wall in sheer frustration and then I cried more because I had possibly fractured my big toe. I couldn't believe that I was going to be here for another five weeks and I didn't have a camera. Not only was it imperative that I took photos of the release site for my TOP report and assessment on Tatok, it was also compulsory for me to have hundreds of excellent photos from any trip I went on for my photo-obsessed mum. Mum would be devastated at having no photos of my time in Sumatra, as would I. She has completed a multitude of photo albums and scrapbooks showcasing my life with animals, whereas the majority of my photos are still on about thirty-seven memory sticks scattered in unknown locations around my disorganised house.

I tried to make myself feel better by playing the 'It could have been worse' game, but the best I could come up with was that Santi could have attacked me when I was on the cage roof and I would have had to be flown home due to horrendous injuries. But hell, at least I would be back home, and at that point in time that was definitely not a bad option. I hated this place. I wanted to go home. I couldn't even ring or email my friends or family for support, since there was no phone or internet at the site. I felt so alone and deflated, and wondered how I was going to cope. I sobbed for another twenty minutes and then somehow managed to compose myself. I went back to the big cage and helped the boys do the final clean. Scrubbing with a broom was good therapy. I then realised that Tatok's large leaves remained where I had dropped them when I had seen Santi with my backpack. Poor

Tatok – after all that, I had forgotten to give him his leaves to play with.

Peter Pratje, the project director, arrived a few days later, so I spent quite a bit of time with him, discussing the release site in general and also my plans for Tatok. Despite trying gallantly to practise my Indonesian with the staff at the release site, it was nice to be able to chat freely with someone in English. I admired Peter for all the work he had done in establishing the release site and for how at ease he felt with Mother Nature. One day I was up at the big cage with Peter when a five-year-old female orangutan named Roberta was put in with Tatok. She had been in isolation for a couple of weeks after being attacked by Santi, but was ready to have some orangutan company again. Peter suggested it would be good to let Tatok out of the cage so he could play in the surrounding trees. He had been let out before and was good at coming back for food. So we opened the cage door and Tatok tentatively made his way out of the cage and climbed a huge ficus tree next to the cage. Out of nowhere, Santi came out of the forest and scaled the same tree Tatok was in. She attacked him and I could hear Tatok screaming and branches shaking. I was screeching from 20 metres below for Santi to leave him alone, but I was helpless to do anything to help poor Tatok.

After about thirty seconds, Tatok came flying down the tree and raced back into the safety of his cage. He had bite wounds on his left foot and right hand. He lay down on the cage floor and started rocking from side to side, his eyes staring blankly through me as I tried to comfort him. I was so angry with Santi and just wished she would piss off. Peter didn't want to move her away from the cage area for a few weeks until fruiting season started, in case she was hungry herself, and also because she had an infant to suckle. I pleaded my case that I couldn't make any progress with Tatok while the cause of his trauma had decided to set up residence a few metres away from his cage.

When I went to the cage early the next morning, Peter had coaxed Santi further into the forest so he could take some photos of her and her infant. Tatok was still traumatised and rocking in the cage. At 10.00 am Puji came and fed the orangutans in the cage and left immediately afterwards to continue his work. The evil Santi must have been watching, because as soon as Puji left, Santi appeared on the cage roof. Tatok went berserk, screaming and climbing frantically in the cage to move to the furthest point away from her. The other orangutans in the cage were also very wary of Santi and watched her intently while trying to eat their sweet potato as quickly as possible so she couldn't steal it. A young male orangutan named Billy was also around the cage area, as he was in pre-release training. Santi suddenly made a beeline for poor Billy. He was terrified, so he started racing away from her. In a stressful situation any young orangutan will immediately rush back to their mother. Well, poor little Billy didn't have a mother, so he ran to the nearest substitute…me! He attached himself to my legs and looked up at me desperately to save him.

So there I was on the slippery platform, with a mouldy rickety staircase leading to the ground 3 metres below and an angry adult female orangutan with a baby rushing towards me. Only one thought entered my brain at that point, and that was 'Run!' I turned around and attempted to make my escape, but there was just one problem – the 15-kilogram ball of traumatised orange fluff attached to my legs, binding them together like I was in a sack race. I hobbled along to the stairs, trying to get Billy to climb up to my torso, but he was like an oyster attached to a rock and there was no moving him. I got to step three and then I slipped, fell on my arse and somehow bumped and slid down the rest of the staircase. I think we actually may have gained a bit of ground by falling down the life-threatening stairs.

Santi proceeded to chase us along the ground for another 20 metres. I knew I couldn't outrun her, so I changed tactics. I turned around, stood my ground and yelled, 'Leave us alone!' It was now a stand-off between two angry young women with a youngster to protect. My chest heaved heavily and sweat was pouring down my face. After about ten seconds, Santi conceded to my bluff and retreated back to the forest. It was a very long ten seconds. Once she was out of sight, Billy climbed up to my chest and gave me what seemed like a big thankyou hug. I breathed a sigh of relief and wrapped my arms around Billy to cuddle him back. I then realised, as I raised my arms, that I had scraped about seven layers of skin off both of my arms in my very ungraceful stair descent.

My injuries were to increase the following day. I was up at the big cage with Peter and OJ, a young female orangutan. OJ loved Peter and they were playing together a lot on the cage platform. She obviously didn't really take a shine to me, because the game she decided to play with me was 'Let's bite Kylie's leg'. She started gently biting my leg and I laughed it off. Then her bite became harder and harder, and I started to worry. It can be very difficult to stop an orangutan from biting you when they basically have four hands and a jaw that can crush human bones. She finally removed her teeth from my leg when Peter told her off. She hadn't broken the skin, but by that night my leg was so bruised and swollen that I could barely put any weight on it.

I woke up with my leg throbbing but made my way to the cage area. After the latest Santi saga two days earlier, it was decided that we would move Tatok down to the small quarantine cage area so he would be away from her. The quarantine cage was about 300 metres away from the large cage complex. I was glad it wasn't too long a walk, since my leg was now mostly purple and green with bruises and still throbbing. I loaded up with treats so I could lure Tatok out of the big cage, through the forest and to the quarantine cage. I was terrified that Tatok would take off and that we would get lost in the forest, but he was a perfect angel and followed me pretty well. He did stop sometimes to eat leaves in the canopy, but some corn and milk proved too tempting on the home stretch and we made it to his new residence in just over an hour.

Later that afternoon, we had some exciting new arrivals. Four orangutans from the Batu Mbelin Quarantine Centre in North Sumatra had arrived, having been deemed suitable for release in the upcoming fruiting season (November–March). Ian Singleton, the conservation director for the Sumatran Orangutan Conservation Programme, and a keeper named Gordon from Jersey Zoo had also come down on the transport. It was great to have some more orangutan nuts to chat with. I had met Ian a couple of times before and he's great value. Ian did his PhD on Sumatran orangutan ranging behaviour and seasonal movements in swamp forest in South Aceh. Peat swamp forest is very difficult to work in, and you are often up to your waist and sometimes shoulders in swamp while taking notes on orangutans living in the luxury of the canopy. Ian's not a big bloke by any stretch of the imagination, but he can outdrink anyone I know and he has a wicked sense of Pommy humour.

Since Ian spent many months tracking orangutans through peat swamps, he thought he was the perfect person to take us on a hike through the forest surrounding the release site the following day – without Peter, who knew this area of forest like the back of his hand. So off I trekked into the forest with Ian, Gordon and Rachmad, the vet from Batu Mbelin. We didn't return to camp for six hours! Ian claimed he wasn't lost, he was simply taking us on the scenic route. Considering Ian had never been to this site before, I didn't see how he knew where the scenic route was. My leg was throbbing, and if I'd known the lovely hike would turn into a death march, I think I would have stayed at the kitchen for a cooking lesson.

We somehow found ourselves climbing up a very steep ravine to return home. Ian led the way and turned around to warn Gordon about some nasty spiky rotan that was in our pathway. Gordon proceeded to turn around and tell me about the spikes ahead as I precariously clung to a 24-centimetre dainty sapling to stop myself sliding back down the ravine we had scaled. I took a few more steps forward and saw the thick rotan stems with spikes sticking out in every direction. I turned my head and warned Rachmad about the rotan just ahead of me. With that I took another step, lost my footing and fell smack bang in the middle of the rotan spikes. I felt like such an idiot. My right forearm took the brunt of the fall and the soft underside of my arm was filled with more than 100 rotan spikes. The larger spikes were sticking out of my flesh and could be pulled out, but many of the smaller spikes had embedded themselves completely under the delicate skin. Surprisingly, it didn't really hurt, and I had to have a good laugh about it since I was stuck on a ravine with my arm looking like a pincushion. My arm was sore and itchy later that night, and even two years later a rash would sometimes appear on my arm where I'm sure the tiny rotan spikes were still living.

Over the next few weeks, I took Tatok out into the forest every day to develop his confidence and forest skills. I also continued with the positive-reinforcement training when he was in the cage. I gave Tatok a lot of love and affection in the short time I spent with him, to try to fill some of the void left by having no mother in his life. People have different views on orangutan rehabilitation and how orphaned orangutans should be treated in order to best equip them for a life back in the wild. Some people believe that tough love is best and that human contact should be kept to a minimum so the orangutan doesn't become dependent on the person in any way. Other people believe that young orangutans do need substitute human affection if they have been orphaned at a young age. I'm definitely a believer of giving love, but it has to be done carefully.

Human children who are brought up in a secure and loving family environment and taught life skills will have more confidence and the ability to succeed later in life and be fully independent when they move out of home. Children who are neglected and forced to do things before they are ready through 'tough love' are often insecure and stressed, and have less chance of success in the real world. I believe the same is true for young orangutans, and this is the approach I took with Tatok. I gave him lots of praise and encouragement for undertaking positive behaviours such as staying in the canopy or foraging for food. If something upset him I would give him some comfort and then encourage him to return to a positive behaviour.

Tatok impressed me greatly with his progress. He rarely came to the ground and seemed content just to check if I was still there occasionally. He was eating a lot, but mostly leaves because there weren't a lot of fruits in the area we were in. I recorded Tatok's behaviour and feeding patterns every two minutes. This is standard protocol for released orangutans being followed at the BTP release site. The data is then entered into a program for analysis. This information is very important, as it gives a clear indication of how an orangutan is performing in the forest. It is vital that a released orangutan spend adequate time feeding and have an acceptable percentage of fruit in their diet to survive in the wild. Released orangutans that are not eating enough wild food will be given supplementary food during the adaptation process. They will also be followed for longer than an orangutan that is doing very well after release.

Tatok was also very good at following me back to his cage when it was time to head home. The fact that I offered him some rice from my lunch if he followed me home may have had something to do with this. One afternoon when I was out with Tatok it started to rain. I bundled my notes into my backpack and tried to take cover under a tree close to Tatok. He proceeded to climb down the tree and onto the path and then started walking quite quickly down one of the cut trails away from the station area. I followed him at a distance and then his walk developed into a run.

A precious cuddle with the troubled Tatok

I called out to him to stop, since I didn't want to move too far into the forest given no one knew where we were.

Suddenly Tatok started somersaulting along the path. Was he having fun? He kept this up for about 30 metres and then moved off the pathway and travelled through the forest for some time. He finally stopped when we came across a small river. He turned around and came back towards me. Suddenly he grabbed my legs and started to climb up my torso. I didn't really know what he was trying to do since he had never initiated physical contact like this. It didn't take long for me to realise that he wanted a proper cuddle and a play session. I couldn't believe it. I started to tickle him and he thought that was fabulous. Tatok tried to protect his belly from being tickled with his knees but he was no match for my fine-tuned tickling skills, and soon all he could do was laugh. Not many things are as satisfying in life to me as making an orangutan laugh – and yes, they can laugh. They will scrunch up their face or do an open-mouth play face and make grunting noises when they are being tickled. After a good tickling session, I proceeded to give Tatok some 'whizzee dizzees'. These involved holding onto his wrists and forearms and spinning him around, just like you would a human toddler.

After all this fun, it was time to try to find our way back to the cage, as it was late afternoon. Now that was easier said than done. My sense of direction is truly abysmal. I get lost in my own local shopping centre, and here I was in a strange forest with one orange dependent and I had no idea where I was. Surprisingly, I managed to stay quite calm. The orangutans in the cages were given their final feed at about 4.00 pm. The technicians loudly banged a piece of bamboo with a stick every time the orangutans at the cages were fed. This was so any orangutans that had been released could return to the area if they were hungry and needed supplementary food while they adapted to living independently in the forest. If all else failed, I could try to follow the sound of the bamboo drum when the orangutans were fed.

I decided to go with my gut and picked a direction. Thankfully, Tatok followed me quite obligingly – I think he was ready for dinner and bed. After a short time I found my way back to a cut trail. Now I had to decide if it was left or right. I picked right and I thought the cage was ahead of me. We kept walking for about ten minutes, and just when I was starting to panic I caught a glimpse of white to my left. I cut back through the forest and found another path, and there was the small cage complex. What a complete fluke! I had gone the wrong way but somehow still found my way back.

Suddenly my time at BTP was nearly over and I began to worry about how Tatok would cope without my guidance. I explained to Peter how much Tatok had improved with gentle coaxing and positive reinforcement. Tatok trusted me, and with that security he could then function in areas he couldn't cope with previously. I showed the technicians how to behave differently when they were around Tatok. This included using gentle body language and speaking quietly. I also asked them to give Tatok food before they began cleaning the cages, as this would keep him occupied while they cleaned and he wouldn't become agitated and rock.

After returning from Sumatra in November, Peter contacted me a few weeks later to let me know that Tatok was doing very well in the forest, and his behaviour had changed dramatically. I was ecstatic and so proud of my little orange fuzz ball. I passed on the good news to Leif, and obviously his mind started ticking. While discussing the release site the following day, Leif said, 'Why don't we release Semeru at BTP when he's about six or seven years old?' With Semeru still only being a baby at this time, I responded with, 'Sounds great', and we chatted about the logistics. It would be in 2011, so we would have ample time to plan and prepare. Or so I thought.

That night I went home and thought excitedly about Semeru's potential for release in the future. By the next day at work, Leif had adjusted his idea somewhat. He said, 'So how about, instead of waiting to release Semeru in 2011, we release Temara instead… next year, in 2006…And you can stay in the jungle with her for a few months and be in charge of her adaptation'. I nearly choked on my apple, but I was never one to shy away from a challenge, so I said, 'Yep, I think we can!' So from this otherwise unremarkable day in December, it became the 'Temara countdown'.

A few months after working with Tatok, I received an email from Peter with his regular update on Tatok while I was at work. I eagerly clicked on it to get an update on his progress. I'm a speed-reader and generally scan things in an email before I digest them properly. I read the words 'We lost Tatok'. I figured that meant Tatok had ventured away from the release site and that they had lost track of him. It only took another second for me to realise that lost was another word for dead. My head started swimming and my eyes pricked with tears. I wanted to close the email and run out of the office, since there were other people around, but I remained glued to the computer screen. I re-read the email and discovered that Tatok had suddenly become very ill in the forest and was dehydrated. The technicians had taken him from the forest and transferred him to one of the 4WDs to rush him back to Jambi City for treatment. Tatok died on the journey out of BTP. A rush of emotions flooded over me – grief and sadness for my poor little Tatok, who had come so far; and panic as to whether this would affect our plans for Temara's future release.

I ran out of the office, down to the primate building and up onto the orangutan roof. Primate staff members know it as the place they can turn to for a private cry – well, private from people anyway. The orangutans tend to take a great interest in someone when they are crying and are fascinated by tears. My best workmates were on a day off since we work on different rosters, so I didn't have anyone to confide in. Of course I told Leif, but what I really needed was a best-girlfriend hug and shoulder to cry on. When I brought the orangutans in that night, they were all on their best behaviour and very quiet because they knew I was upset. Utama sat quietly with me as I sobbed and rested my head on the mesh of her night den. She had no words to comfort me, but she poked her index finger through the mesh and gently wiped my tears and touched my hair as I thought about my beloved Tatok dying on the back of a dirty 4WD and leaving his jungle home forever.

7

The chosen one

I knew that I would always hold Tatok's memory with me, but I now had to focus all of my energy on preparing Temara for her history-making journey to the jungles of her true home in Sumatra. News of Temara's impending release spread through Perth Zoo and zoos throughout Australasia. The proposal was met with excitement, curiosity and, of course, as with any bold event in history, criticism. Some people felt strongly that a zoo-born orangutan would not be able to adapt to living in the wild. These people had not met Temara! The mental health of an orangutan is the key component in determining whether they will be able to adapt to a different environment and learn new strategies and skills. Temara was chosen for release based on her sex, age and physical health, but mostly on her personality and mental health.

Temara was raised naturally by her mother, Puteri, and she experienced a secure and nurturing upbringing. She also lived with her older half-sister, Utama, for many years. When it was decided to transport her to Sumatra, Temara was thirteen years old and at the age she would naturally leave her mother in the wild. Temara was also independent and did not seek out contact or affection from the orangutan keepers. She was an active orangutan, highly intelligent, and showed excellent problem-solving skills. She ate a wide variety of food and was definitely not a fussy eater, as she had learnt from her food-ingesting vacuum-cleaner mother, Puteri.

Perth Zoo has a very high standard of care for the orangutans. We have one of the best breeding programs in the world. In fact, twenty-nine orangutan infants have been born at the zoo. Orangutans at Perth Zoo also live well into their forties, and our oldest female, named Puan, is more than sixty years old. The enclosures and care provided for the Perth Zoo orangutans promote natural behaviours they would undertake in the wild. These include nest building, foraging and tool use. Orangutans are kept in their natural social units. Female orangutans live with one or two offspring and they are raised naturally by their mothers. Young orangutans are only separated from their mother at the natural age of dispersion. A loving and nurturing upbringing will help ensure that the young orangutan is confident and independent after leaving its mother. Temara had the opportunity to observe Sekara raising her infant Semeru in the adjoining exhibit. We felt that this would improve Temara's chance of being a successful first-time mother in the Sumatran rainforest.

The climbing structures and ropes in the Perth Zoo orangutan exhibits mimic the flexible branches and vines of the rainforest canopy well. All the orangutans there spend the majority of their time on the arboreal platforms and rarely come to the ground.

Due to Temara's sound psychological health, high intelligence and independent personality, Leif and I strongly believed that she

Temara in a contemplative mood at Perth Zoo (Photo: Derek Smith)

was well equipped to handle the transition from a zoo environment to the rainforests of Sumatra. She was already competent in many skills needed to live in the forest. It was expected that her intelligence and curiosity would encourage her to explore the forest, travel, construct sleeping nests and eat a variety of food, including leaves. Her wariness of humans and independent nature would hopefully encourage her to move away from the release station over time and not be reliant on the trackers for extra food.

Even though Leif and I believed that transitioning Temara to a jungle life was possible, an abundance of discussions, meetings, phone calls and emails ensued, to present our proposal and obtain approval from the relevant people and government departments. As it was a world first, Leif and I prepared detailed documentation of how we would undertake Temara's release, and highlighted the experience and success rate of the orangutan release program at BTP. Perth Zoo CEO Susan Hunt and the zoo board were supportive of this world-first proposal, and shared our vision to release Temara and protect the precious habitat of BTP. The Perth Zoo ethics committee and the Western Australian Minister for the Environment also approved the release, after studying our proposal and discussing all the issues involved. Staff travel, including my extended stay in the jungle to assist with Temara's adaptation to the wild, was also approved.

Zoos have many regulations that need to be followed when it comes to the transportation of animals to other zoos or release into the wild. Perth Zoo has an amazing reputation for the breeding and release of many native species into the wild, including the Western swamp tortoise, dibbler and numbat. However, Perth Zoo had never released an orangutan into the wild. In fact, no zoo in the world had, so with that came an abundance of further communication with zoo officials. This included the orangutan species coordinator for the Australasian region. Our zoo registrar began work on obtaining multiple permits for Temara's travel, both at a regional and international level. As well, we had to ensure that we were following the guidelines of the International Union for Conservation of Nature (IUCN) – the world's oldest and largest global environmental organisation.

Thankfully for my sanity, I wasn't heavily involved with the permit and regulation side of things. I was, however, in charge of Temara's preparation for her monumental journey. We separated Temara from her mother, Puteri, in April 2006 when Temara was thirteen years old. Both orangutans coped very well with the separation, since a female orangutan would normally leave her mother by about the age of eleven in the wild. Personally, I think Puteri was relieved to have some quiet time, because Temara was a rambunctious and challenging teenager. Changes were introduced to Temara's diet in preparation for a jungle menu. She was given more frequent but smaller meals throughout the day, to mimic the constant ranging and foraging behaviour of wild orangutans. She was also given more leaves to eat and offered live food, such as termites. She didn't show much of an appreciation for the creepy-crawlies and looked at them as if she was above eating such things.

In July, Temara was moved into an exhibit that had a large ficus tree. This tree had a large metal sleeve around the base of the trunk so orangutans could not climb it and destroy the tree. Even in the jungle, orangutans can cause a lot of damage to the trees in which they forage and nest. The luxury of living in the jungle compared to a zoo is that orangutans are constantly on the move and the trees have time to recover.

Temara was given a surprise in September when we attached ropes from her main artificial climbing tower into the ficus tree canopy. Surprisingly, Temara did not venture into the tree canopy for at least five days after we attached the ropes – well, at least not during keepers' working hours. I was disappointed, since Temara had always been so quick to try new things. I was lucky enough, though, to be the first one to see her in the tree. I was coming back from lunch and walking down the driveway towards the primate building when I heard a rustling noise from Temara's exhibit and looked up. At that moment the rustling stopped, but I spotted a flash of orange hair in the tree. Temara then peered down at me from behind some foliage, looking sheepish as if she had just been caught in the act of doing something she wasn't supposed to. I proceeded to praise Temara and called other primate keepers on my two-way radio to come and see Temara in the tree. Temara thought this was completely unacceptable and proceeded to throw a tantrum and climbed out of the tree as quickly as possible.

The ficus tree was used in Temara's pre-release training. We wanted Temara to relate climbing and foraging in the tree canopy to finding food, since she would need to source all her food in trees once she was living in the jungle. As well as the usual figs the ficus tree contained, we wanted to make it even more attractive. This is why I invented the 'flying fruit nunchuk'. This involved using an apple corer to put a hole through various fruits, including apples, pears and oranges. I would then feed a short length of rope through the hole in the fruit and tie a knot at either end to keep the fruit secure. The problem was then trying to get the fruit up into the 15-metre-high tree. My first attempt resulted in me giving myself a partial concussion as I tried to lasso the fruit nunchuk above my head and hoist it up into the tree while I was in the exhibit and Temara was locked inside. I somehow managed to slam the apple and orange into my forehead as I was attempting the upward throw. Thank God this exhibit was not on display for the general public, or I would have ended up on *Australia's Funniest Home Videos*.

Later in the day I decided to try a different method of getting the fruit nunchuk in the tree. I went up onto the primate building roof. I was now about 8 metres away from the tree canopy, but I was also a lot higher up, so it seemed promising. Temara was up on the climbing frame out in the exhibit, and she watched with curiosity as I again lassoed the nunchuk above my head and hoisted it towards the ficus tree in the exhibit. She then looked with great interest as the fruit nunchuk hit a branch and fell to the ground. Within about eight seconds, Temara had raced down the climbing frame, collected the free food and then proceeded to eat it once she was back up the climbing frame. This was not going well. In my attempt to encourage Temara to forage in the ficus tree, I had given myself a killer headache and given her free food – on the ground!

I came up with the perfect way to get the fruit nunchuk in the tree the following day. While Temara was still in her night den eating her breakfast, I asked Mark, a 185-centimetre primate keeper, to assume the flying-fruit-nunchuk-wielding position on the roof. I waited in Temara's exhibit near the tree. Mark would then attempt to hoist the nunchuk into the tree. If he missed then I could collect it and throw it back up to him on the keepers' platform. For the first few days, by the time Mark got the fruit into the tree, it was quite bruised after a few heavy landings. But he got the knack of it pretty quickly, and I improved greatly as well, so we could soon throw the fruit nunchuks into the tree throughout the day, to encourage Temara to forage in the tree canopy. Occasionally I would have an uncoordinated throw and Temara would get a free feed on the ground while I did the walk of shame back to the office.

Temara also used the tree to gather nesting material, so she could build a nest on the climbing frame. This was very positive. The ultimate would have been if Temara actually made a nest in the tree, but she chose the more comfortable option, being the smart orangutan she is, so I wasn't too worried. Orangutans generally make nests in the wild in tree forks or on interconnecting branches that provide structural support. They will then fold small branches inwards to form the base of a nest and add other small leafy branches for extra comfort. Temara showed that she could challenge any wild-born orangutan in a nest-building competition. She constructed a large nest from ficus branches on the top of her climbing structure. She would sit in this nest, 12 metres above the ground, and have a view of the entire zoo grounds. She added new branches and foliage to it daily, so the nest soon became massive. It was a talking point among zoo staff, since it could be seen from a great distance.

Temara very rarely came to the ground in any exhibit she was in. It is imperative that released orangutans do not view the ground as an appropriate place to be. The critically endangered Sumatran tiger is a formidable predator that is best avoided by being high in the canopy. It was very positive that Temara already viewed the ground as an undesirable place.

Leif and I began to go into the exhibit with Temara on a regular basis to feed her, since we were the ones accompanying her to Sumatra. These visits were to accustom Temara to obtaining food from her keepers. We accepted that Temara would probably need supplementary food after her release, as she became used to her new jungle environment and learnt how to find various forest food. Temara was going to be followed by one or two Indonesian trackers who worked at the release site, and they would give Temara her extra food ration. We therefore needed Temara to be able to come down low in the canopy to accept this food. I would also speak to Temara with a few key Indonesian words that the trackers would use with her. These included *makan* for 'eat' and *naik* for 'climb'.

Training Temara to take food from me while on the climbing frame

Temara was required to have a pre-export examination by the veterinary team before leaving for Sumatra. She was anaesthetised for this and given a thorough check-over by our senior vet Simone. She was also given numerous vaccinations, including measles/mumps/rubella, polio, rabies and tetanus.

Temara, being the highly intelligent and slightly suspicious orangutan she is, seemed to sense that something was going on in the weeks leading up to her departure, and she stopped coming into her night den in the afternoons. All orangutans at Perth Zoo come into their night dens in the late afternoon to be fed and secured inside. While in the winter months they are kept inside and go to sleep by 5.00 pm, in summer the keepers will keep the orangutans inside for a short period of time in the late afternoon and then put food in various puzzle feeders outside for them. The orangutans are then given access to both the outside exhibit and night den, and can choose where they wish to sleep in the warmer weather.

Since it was spring, Temara was reluctant to enter her night den, even for a short time, due to the lovely weather. But we needed to be able to secure her inside her night den before leaving for Indonesia, since she had to be anaesthetised on the day of her departure and placed in her transport crate. Orangutan keepers started to stress when Temara, out of the blue, decided that she was not going to enter her den any more when keepers were there, so she couldn't be locked inside. As soon as the orangutan keepers left for the day and Temara saw them walking up to the office, she would climb down and enter the den for her dinner because she knew the keepers could not lock her in! This went on for more than a week, and D-day was looming. In desperation, the orangutan keepers devised a cunning plan in an attempt to outsmart Temara.

We set up a mirror system where we could see if Temara had entered the den but she couldn't see us. On the afternoon we planned to secure Temara in her den, we had to sneak our supervisor, Clare, into the night-den complex from a back entrance so that Temara didn't see her. The orangutan keepers then had to lock up the building and walk up to the office so Temara thought everything was normal and we had all gone home. Temara watched us walk up to the office from her high vantage point and then we saw her climb down from the top platform in her quest to head into the night den for her dinner.

Poor Clare had to hide in the storeroom next to Temara's night den and watch the small wall-mounted mirror we had set up so we could see Temara's reflection when she entered the den. Clare had to hold her arm out at shoulder height with her finger ready on the button to close the pneumatic sliding door that would shut Temara inside. Temara only took about three minutes to enter the den, but for Clare it seemed like an eternity. Her arm started to turn to jelly and then it went completely numb. Clare later confessed that she had the sudden realisation that the message from her brain might in fact not connect to her button-pressing finger, since she could no longer feel her arm! She was also trying not to breathe too loudly or give off any negative vibes, in case Temara could sense her hidden in the storeroom. The other primate keepers and I were all in the office pacing or biting our nails in nervous anticipation. Temara finally entered the den and Clare shut the slide in time so that Temara was secured inside. Temara was not impressed, but we all came back down to the area and gave her lots of food treats and apologies. We all agreed that being locked inside for two days was a worthwhile sacrifice in exchange for the rest of her life in the open jungle!

8

Journey to Sumatra

Our departure date for Sumatra was 31 October 2006. The flight left at 10.30 am, but when an animal needs to board the plane, the day needs to start a lot earlier. I think I was more stressed a week before we left for Sumatra than the actual night before our departure. I have always been like that. I will stress constantly about something and then just before the event a strange calm will set in. Maybe the shot or two of port I had before going to bed also helped. We arrived at the zoo at 5.00 am, just as dawn was breaking through the night sky. All of the orangutan exhibits were cleaned and the orangutans were let outside – except for Temara, of course. Temara was not impressed. At 6.00 am, Simone, the senior vet, arrived at the building to anaesthetise Temara so she could be put into her transport crate. Again, Temara was not impressed.

Temara was sedated quickly and placed in her very well-padded transport crate. She was only given a very light anaesthetic so she would be fully recovered in time for her international flight. Clare and Martina were responsible for transporting Temara to the airport in an enclosed vehicle. They had special tarmac access passes so they could stay with Temara right up until the moment she was transferred into the plane's cargo hold. Leif and I went to the airport separately so we could check in as normal passengers. Perth Zoo's CEO, Susan, was also travelling to Jakarta with us for the official welcome ceremony for Temara. Leif and I would then continue on with Temara to Jambi City and then the jungle.

An Australian film crew was also going to travel to BTP on 15 November in order to film Temara's release the following day. They decided to film her departure from Perth, so they were on the tarmac as Temara was loaded onto the plane at Perth Airport. I had my face pressed up against the large viewing windows, watching as Clare and Martina said their goodbyes to Temara though the mesh of the crate. Clare had her arm around Martina and I could see Martina's shoulders shaking. I knew she was crying. I had to turn away from the window since my own eyes started to prick with tears. We boarded shortly afterwards and as the plane sped down the runway and made its way upwards, I closed my eyes and thought, 'There's no going back now!' I needed some reassurance as the reality of the huge task ahead began to sink in. My close zoo friends had given me cards and letters to open on the plane, so I delved into my backpack to retrieve the letters and hungrily read their messages of support.

We landed in Jakarta in the mid-afternoon. Peter Pratje was at the airport waiting for us. Temara was transferred to a large, secure hangar just outside the airport. We all travelled with her to meet some officials and go through the procedure for the welcome ceremony and media the following day. Temara had to stay in her transport crate in this building overnight. This wouldn't have been so bad, but there happened to be about twenty other people in the same room setting up for the welcome ceremony. This included putting up curtains, setting out chairs and constructing a massive wooden sign. All of this activity was very noisy. At this point I was beginning to wish I had learnt some Indonesian swear words. I was so annoyed that this work had not been done earlier, as Temara should have been in a dark and quiet room. Thankfully, Temara remained calm and quiet in her crate and took food and fluids from me.

Leif, Peter and Susan left the hangar at about 7.00 pm and went out for dinner with some Indonesian officials. I refused to leave Temara until the room had been set up and everyone had left. I thought this would only take a couple of hours. I was so very wrong. I didn't leave the hangar until after midnight, and I was tired and starving! There was a massive thunderstorm at about 9.00 pm, and this caused traffic chaos in the city. Material for the display board was being couriered over to the hangar as the storm hit and was then delayed by more than two hours. So I spent more than five hours sitting on the floor, guarding Temara's crate and giving death stares to anyone who made too much noise or tried to look in the crate. I also ate half a mango from Temara's goodie bag, since it was the only dinner I was going to get. The material eventually arrived at close to midnight, and the final touches to the room were made. By this time Temara looked extremely tired but I was grateful that she had remained calm and not had a tantrum like I nearly did. I managed to get to the hotel and stagger into bed by about 1.00 am, too tired to stress about the busy day ahead.

The following day proved quite chaotic. The welcome ceremony and media event began at 9.00 am at the airport. We arrived at about 7.00 am so I could check on Temara and give her fluids and food, which she took. A large number of journalists

Welcome sign in place after midnight construction

and photographers arrived for the welcome ceremony, and we were surrounded by excited chatter and camera flashes. Temara was moved to a nearby room before the ceremony commenced. I, of course, was practically glued to the crate to keep a watchful eye on her. Numerous photographers approached me, wanting to see Temara. I had a blanket covering the crate and I explained to them that it was impossible to see her properly through the mesh, even when I removed the blanket. To my horror, they were then quite persistent in suggesting that I let Temara out of the crate so they could photograph her. I knew then that they obviously didn't understand that Temara was a large adult female orangutan and was incredibly strong. They must have had images of me opening the crate and gently holding a cute 3-kilogram ball of baby orangutan fuzz. I had to then explain that if I did in fact open the crate, a very annoyed 45-kilogram giant ball of fuzz would come hurtling out of the crate, break their cameras and cause the airport to be shut down due to a tarmac security breach.

The welcome ceremony lasted for approximately thirty minutes, and numerous speeches and presentations of gifts were made. Framed photographs of Temara were given as gifts, but unfortunately the photograph used, which was also included on the welcome poster, was quite unflattering. Temara's crate was then loaded onto a vehicle to depart for the domestic airport. By this time Temara was very subdued and was also quite hot. I pretty much felt the same way, and I just wanted to get to BTP. The next part of the journey was a one-hour plane flight from Jakarta to Jambi. A police helicopter was waiting at Jambi Domestic Airport to transport us to the release site. We didn't want Temara to have to endure the crazy road trip into BTP, so Leif and Peter had spent a great amount of time organising a helicopter flight. By this stage I was worried about Temara because she was extremely subdued and refused food and fluids.

The helicopter flight to the release site was forty-five minutes. Despite being a bit nervous, I still tried to enjoy the view as we headed towards Temara's new home. She was transferred into a quarantine cage at the release site as soon as we arrived in the early afternoon. She came out of the crate immediately and stretched after such a long journey, then ate and took fluids, and made a sleeping nest that night with leaves and a Qantas blanket she had taken out of the transport crate. It was such a relief that we were over the first hurdle, which was getting Temara to the remote release site in the first place. I stayed with her until she had eaten and settled in her nest. She looked tired and had a scratch on her forehead, but apart from that she looked okay and seemed quite calm.

Temara arrives at BTP via police helicopter

I went and had some dinner up at the little kitchen and chatted to Leif and Peter about Temara's upcoming release. My chilli tolerance was much improved since my last trip, and I had a big dinner of rice, vegetables, fish and chilli. Leif and I were staying in the vet clinic, and I even managed to get my same trusty old room, which proved quite comforting. Unfortunately, it still had the old dirty and holey mosquito net, so I took my malaria tablet, put on some insect repellent and went to bed.

Due to quarantine regulations, Temara had to remain in the quarantine cage for two weeks before she was allowed to be released. She had enough room to walk around and stretch out, but she was not used to being locked inside every day. I tried to explain to her that we wouldn't bring her all this way only to lock her in a cage and that in two weeks, the jungle would be her new playground. In some way I think that Temara understood. When she saw a young orangutan playing in the trees close to her cage, I hoped she realised that she too would soon have that chance.

During Temara's quarantine she was introduced to her two trackers, named Herman and Perizal. Both were young men in their early twenties but they were very different. Herman was quite loud, smiley and enjoyed singing while he worked. Perizal was shy and very softly spoken. He also looked like he was about fourteen years old. I spent a lot of time with Herman and Perizal, and showed them how to behave around Temara. Sadly for Herman, this meant toning down his singing, since Temara was not a fan of the loud *Indonesian Idol* wannabe. I showed the boys some positive-reinforcement training sessions with Temara and they seemed quite impressed. I also explained Temara's behaviour and what caused her to become upset. Herman and Perizal learnt quickly and were soon speaking softly to Temara and hand-feeding her without being grabbed. They were given Perth Zoo uniforms to wear, so Temara quickly became accustomed to receiving food from people in the familiar green uniform. It was imperative that Temara knew and trusted her trackers for the first stage of her release, in case she needed to be led to a different area and also to receive supplementary food if required.

While Temara slowly grew more accustomed to Herman and Perizal, there was another technician that both she and I didn't particularly like. He was at the station when I worked with Tatok, and he would always laugh at me and mimic my voice. Apparently, even Indonesian people think I sound like Alvin the Chipmunk. I pointed the technician out to Leif after a few days and told him I wasn't fond of him. Leif nicknamed him Big Hair because he had big, boofy pretty-boy Indonesian-style hair and thought he was a supermodel. Temara would attempt to hit the technicians, including Big Hair, while they were cleaning her cage, and they were terrified of her. I couldn't help but be amused when Big Hair went to put some pineapple on the ledge of the cage for Temara and she tried to grab him. Big Hair squealed like Alvin the Chipmunk, stepped back and dropped the food in fright. I swallowed my smirk as Big Hair sheepishly picked up the food and gave it to me to feed Temara.

Herman and Perizal collected forest fruits for Temara while she was in quarantine so she could sample what her future forest Sizzler bar would have on offer. Many people think the rainforest is full of large, luscious and sweet fruits, but these are a rarity. Most forest fruits are quite small and bitter. Many fruits require quite a lot of work to get to an energy-dense seed in the middle. Temara was not very impressed with many of the items that were offered to her. I would eat the fruits in front of her and act as if they tasted like luscious mango to encourage her to eat them, but she wasn't fooled. She did eat some of the fruits, though, including ficus, which is a rainforest staple, so that was positive.

Temara was also given large leaves in the late afternoon for nesting material, and she didn't disappoint. She would make an intricate nest every evening at the back of the cage and settle down to sleep. Other young orangutans that were being looked after at the station were also brought within visual range of Temara's cage. This allowed Temara to observe other orangutans interacting with the BTP staff and also watch them climb and forage in the nearby trees.

During Temara's quarantine, Leif and I spent a lot of time becoming familiar with the marked trail system at the release site with Peter, who knew the trails very well. Multiple interlinking trails had been established at the release site so the staff could use them to travel through the forest more efficiently. These trails were marked with red paint on a tree every 10 metres. Every 50 metres there was a metal tag with the trail name (e.g. Trail Z) and the number in metres of where you were on the trail. The technicians used these trail systems in the dark of early morning to trek out to the orangutan they had followed on the previous day. When the technician was close to the orangutan, he would leave the track, head into the forest and wait under the nesting tree of the orangutan. When the orangutan wakes and begins to travel, the technician can follow it. I'm always amazed how the technicians find their way so easily and know which tree the orangutan is nesting in. To me, all the trees look the same in the dark.

Undertaking Jungle Orientation 101 classes with Peter and Leif was challenging. Peter was extremely physically fit and confident in the jungle. I viewed him as the German version of G.I. Joe. Leif wasn't as fit as Peter, but he has very long legs, so trekking through the jungle with these two was like boot camp. On top of that, I was made to navigate using a compass and GPS unit so they could be confident I would have the skills to find my way home if I was separated from the trackers after the release. I was relieved to have these items with me in the jungle due to my absolutely useless sense of direction. At least if I got lost after Temara's release I had a slightly higher chance of survival with these trusty tools.

Despite being in the depths of the Sumatran jungle, we managed to get email! Before we left Perth, the Perth Zoo computer technicians set up a satellite email system on our laptop. We had to experiment to find the best place to pick up a signal at the vet clinic, and it would often cut out in the middle of an email, so we quickly learnt to write up any long emails we wanted to send in a Word document and save as we went. Then, when we had a good connection, we would just cut and paste our text into the email to save a lot of time, frustration and swearing at the laptop. It was so nice to be able to have some contact with my friends and family back home. I would keep them up to date with what was happening in BTP and they would always be supportive and encouraging. It was also great to hear about the other orangutans at Perth Zoo, because of course I missed them.

Whenever we used the laptop at night, the screen would be covered in a plague of flying ants – scientific name unknown. Their purpose in life seemed to be to track down the nearest light source, enter the building, drop all of their wings and then slowly die. In fact, there was a multitude of various insect plagues during my time at BTP, and some of them seemed to be of biblical proportions.

I had found my five weeks at this release site in 2005 challenging, and this time it was going to be for three months. Despite people always saying I'm a friendly and outgoing person, I really am a bit of a homebody, and I have always been very prone to homesickness. While other kids at school loved school camps, I used to cry myself to sleep at night because I was homesick. Once I even slept in the same room as one of my teachers because I was keeping everyone awake with my sobbing. Even as an adult, while travelling, I will always think about home, especially my pets, who don't understand why I leave them. My parents always look after my dog, Cooper, while I'm in Indonesia and spoil him rotten. He is walked more, fed more, patted more and generally showered with more love, because at least one of my parents is usually home during the day. As soon as I get back from my travels and go to my parents' house to pick Cooper up, though, he won't even look at my parents. He turns his head the other way when they talk to him, for fear that they want to keep him forever. He won't leave my side and waits outside the toilet door if I have to go – which can be quite often after returning from Indonesia. Having email contact meant I could check on how Cooper was going, which was a great relief.

Soon after our arrival at BTP, I began to get itchy. Very itchy! When my older brother Michael was little he was always the sick and allergic one; he had eczema, rashes and numerous food allergies. For Easter, Mum used to get us carob chocolate, since Michael was allergic to dairy products. I thought carob was disgusting. I was not impressed with my substandard Easter goody basket, despite my mother's good intentions of providing my brother with a supportive little sister during the chocolate-eating season. Then there was the weird soap he had to use for his sensitive skin, which I had to use too if we were having a bath together when we were really little. It was yellow, smelt weird and was the size of a house brick! My poor mum also had to buy white cotton bedsheets so she could cut them up and use them as bandages on Michael's itchy and bloodied skin.

Somehow, the older my brother got, the healthier he became. His allergies disappeared and he rarely got sick. I think he passed his festy torch to me, since as I got older I developed hayfever, other sicknesses and very sensitive skin. It's bad enough having sensitive skin in Western Australia's warm, dry climate, but having skin allergies in humid Indonesia made me a walking petri dish for weird tropical skin conditions. I had bites all over me and I then developed an all-over body rash. They drove me absolutely crazy, and none of my creams or medications could calm the angry Sumatran welts. They itched the most when I was in bed, but I think that was because it was all I could think about as I lay there in the dark with the rain beating down on the roof. I would scratch so much that the bites would begin to bleed and then throb. I told my friends and family this on email just so I could have a whinge and vent, but my darling mother is always proactive, so she printed out my email and pleaded for an immediate appointment with our family doctor. She came out with a prescription for some potent creams that she could send over to me with the film crew.

So it was with great anticipation that I awaited the film crew's arrival on 15 November. Not only would that mark the day before Temara's release, but it also meant that possible relief for my tropical itch was in store. The film crew consisted of a lovely reporter named Andrea, a cameraman and a sound technician. Unlike us, they didn't have the luxury of a helicopter ride out to the site, and upon arrival they were exhausted from the rough road trip into the release station. A German girl named Sabine had also arrived on the transport with the film crew. She was going to stay at the site for about six weeks to undertake orangutan observations. It was nice to know that I would have someone to have girly chats with once I was the only one left from Perth with Temara in the harsh Sumatran jungle.

Leif and I spent the day doing interviews with the film crew about Temara and how we felt about being involved in this world-first event. I felt excited, nervous, determined and physically ill all at the same time when I thought about opening Temara's cage door in less than twenty-four hours. It was hard to believe that the time had almost come. I spent a long time with Temara that afternoon as she prepared her sleeping nest for her last night in quarantine. I hoped this would be the last time in her life that she would sleep in a cage or captivity of any sort. Tomorrow night she would be sleeping in a tree, under the stars and in the jungle of her home country. I only wished that I could explain this to her, since she was beginning to appear pretty fed up with her new living quarters. She had gone from a four-star accommodation rating at Perth Zoo to a measly 1.5 stars in her small quarantine cage.

Not only did I feel bad about Temara being in the quarantine cage, I then had to apologise to her for stealing her precious blanket. Temara had kept the blue Qantas blanket with her in the quarantine cage ever since she was transferred from the transport crate. Qantas often donates old blankets to the zoo for us to use for animal bedding. The orangutans love their blankets, and even on a hot day they will often be seen with a blanket over their head. I asked Herman to distract Temara with some food and then in one quick motion I shoved my arm up through the cage bars and wrenched the dirty and foul-smelling blanket out of the cage. Temara spun around and reached out her arm in an effort to save her blankie but it was too late. I swear she gave me a dirty look, but I offered her some food treats to try to make it up to her. I didn't think it would be appropriate if Temara's first moments in the wild captured on film included footage of her with a dirty blanket trailing behind her like a wedding veil.

I gave Temara a pep talk about being careful the next day and explained that she'd have to be tough. I started to get a bit teary, because as much as I believed this was the right thing to do and Temara had a very high chance of success, just like any devoted parent saying goodbye to their grown child as they embark on a daring adventure, I couldn't help but worry. In true Temara style, she seemed quite indifferent to my emotional plea and lay down to go to sleep. With a satisfied smile, I bade Temara goodnight so she could get a sound night's sleep in preparation for the following history-making day.

At least Temara got some sleep! I have insomnia at the best of times, so let's just say there was never a hope in hell of me sleeping well the night before we released Temara into the jungle.

I did have some relief from my itchiness, though, since I lathered myself in three different creams my mum had sent up. I couldn't decide which one to use, so I tried the creams on different areas of my body rash in an experiment to see which one worked best. As well as the creams for my bites and rashes, Mum had also managed to sneak some chocolate into my supplies bag. And not just any chocolate! This was Swiss chocolate with kirsch. So even though I barely slept, at least I was slightly less itchy and had chocolate and kirsch in my belly.

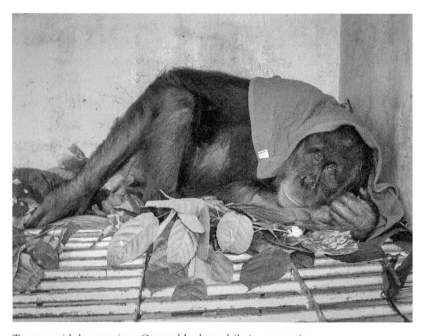

Temara with her precious Qantas blanket while in quarantine

9

Temara meets the jungle

Morning finally arrived and my chest was tight with anticipation after my restless night. We met for breakfast at 7.00 am and I forced myself to eat some noodles, knowing that it would be a very long day with no time to stop for food. We then packed all our supplies, including water, insect repellent, raincoats, camera, binoculars, notepad, pens and food for Temara. We were hoping Temara would stay within the trail system around the release site for at least a few weeks, so we could come back to the station at night to eat and sleep, but we had brought tents and thin blow-up mattresses with us in case we needed to camp out in the jungle.

We met at Temara's cage at 10.00 am. Temara seemed quite suspicious of all of the people at her cage that morning chatting animatedly and setting up camera equipment. She knew something was up, so I stayed close to her and spoke gently to keep her calm. Both Herman and Perizal were going to follow Temara for the first few days. There would also be Leif, Peter, the film crew and me. We had told the film crew that depending on how Temara went, we might have to ask them to hold back or go back to camp, as we didn't want Temara becoming stressed.

At 10.51 am, Leif and I both opened the door to Temara's cage. It seemed only fitting that the two people who had mainly worked with Temara since she was born now held open the door to her freedom. I felt totally calm at this point, and my quiet sense of confidence was growing. We had laid bets as to how long it would take Temara to actually leave the safety of the cage. I said she would come out in less than five minutes. Temara didn't disappoint me. She came over to the door immediately after it was opened and ventured out of the cage within thirty seconds. She tested the rubber rope that led from the cage to a nearby large tree, then used both hands and feet to quickly scale the rubber rope and within a few seconds was perched in a tree fork 15 metres above us, assessing her new-found freedom. Temara spent the next hour travelling in the trees close to the cage area. She even came back to the cage twice, since it was all she had known for the past fortnight and it was familiar. I bit my lower lip nervously whenever Temara tested branches and vines before moving to another tree. The canopy was quite poor in this area, but Temara looked like a wild orangutan as she climbed in the canopy and tested her travel route before letting go of her secure hand- or foothold.

At 12.10 pm there was a sudden change of pace. Temara suddenly went to the ground and bolted. We all took off after her, with Herman and Perizal leading the charge. I was soon left behind by Temara and the Indonesian boys, who moved like the wind in the jungle. I switched my following technique from watching the trackers to listening to the sound of breaking vegetation ahead of me, since I wasn't quick enough to keep Temara or her trackers in my line of sight. We all managed to meet up after about ten minutes, when Temara climbed another tree. Herman and Perizal had never lost sight of Temara, and appeared perfectly calm. I was in the early stages of a panic attack, since I thought we were going to lose Temara, while Leif was red and sweaty from keeping up on the chase. Suddenly what we were doing seemed very real and quite overwhelming. We sent the film crew back to the station, since they couldn't keep up due to the extensive equipment they had to carry. We also didn't want to stress Temara with too many people following her, and obviously her needs came first.

Temara went to the ground a couple more times in the afternoon and ran. There were lots of bees around in the forest, and at one point Temara was chased for a short time by a swarm of them, which was quite stressful for her. She settled by mid-afternoon and took food from Leif and me, which was a relief. I had also brought fluids for her, which she took readily. With the humid climate and extended physical activity Temara was now undertaking, I didn't want her to become dehydrated on the first day of her release.

Temara impressed us greatly in the late afternoon by feeding extensively on two different forest fruits. Her feeding continued well past the time most wild orangutans have built a nest and settled down to sleep for the night. At 6.15 pm it started to become dark very quickly. As darkness rapidly approached, Temara suddenly became agitated. She began to shake branches and climbed lower down in the canopy to check what we were all doing. It seemed as if she had suddenly realised that it was nearly dark, she was in a strange place and she didn't know where to sleep. She kiss-squeaked in annoyance and seemed to be contemplating going to the ground. A kiss-squeak is a very distinctive sound made by an orangutan when they are annoyed or stressed. In simple terms, it sounds like a person blowing raspberries. A word of advice: if you

Checking on Temara during her early jungle days

ever visit orangutans at a zoo or are ever lucky enough to see them in the wild, do not make cute kissing noises at them, as humans and orangutans interpret this sound quite differently.

We were determined not to let Temara descend the tree, since if she ran on the ground in the dark, we would certainly lose her. Temara then had to experience some tough love from the five people below her. We all began banging on the tree she was in and yelling at her to climb back into the canopy and make a sleeping nest. I felt terrible doing this, but having Temara annoyed at us up in a tree was a far better outcome than a lost orangutan on her first night in the jungle. Temara reluctantly got the message pretty quickly and climbed back into the canopy. She moved into different trees and after a few minutes we could hear the sound of small branches being broken and hoped she was building a nest. Unfortunately, Temara wasn't in a very good tree, but we didn't want to coax her into a larger tree, as it was nearly dark. By 7.00 pm Temara had been quiet for over ten minutes, so we quietly left the area and made the trek back to the station.

We all went straight back to the kitchen so we could update the film crew on Temara's afternoon exploits and tuck into some much-sought-after dinner. Leif had somehow managed to bring a bottle of red wine with him to the release site. We filled our classy plastic cups and merrily toasted Temara's first day in the jungle. I couldn't wipe the smile off my face, but I was also worried about her first night in the jungle by herself. My empathy for Temara would cause me many a sleepless night during my time at BTP, and this first night was of course one of them.

It didn't really matter that I didn't sleep that night, since we had to get up at 4.30 am anyway in order to make it to Temara's nest by 5.30 am. When tracking an orangutan in the jungle, you need to arrive at their nesting site before they start travelling for the day or you will never find them. We arrived at Temara's nesting tree at 5.33 am. Temara made her first formal appearance for the day at 11.30 am, six hours after we arrived at her nesting tree. We knew she was in the canopy resting, as the trackers spotted her quite quickly, but she did not move out of her nest until 11.30 am and didn't start travelling until 12.30 pm. I wouldn't have been surprised if she had experienced a restless and uncomfortable night, and she was probably in need of a sleep-in. At least Temara had the luxury of being able to sleep in, I thought as I contemplated putting matchsticks in my eye sockets to keep my eyes open.

Temara had a reasonably lazy second day in the jungle and didn't eat as much forest fruit as on her first day, but she also rarely came to the ground, which was very positive. Leif and I also gave her

112

supplementary food and fluids. Unfortunately, she made the same mistake of leaving her nest building until very late. She became agitated at 5.30 pm and kept looking at us on the ground. She began moving through the canopy, but was bordering on having a tantrum, as we surrounded every tree she occupied to prevent her coming down and making a run for it on the ground. She proceeded to fluff about up in the canopy until just after 6.00 pm but then became quiet. It was becoming reasonably dark and we were about to let out a sigh of relief when Temara started to climb down her tree. The five of us were quite vocal in telling her to get back into that canopy quick smart or else, and thankfully she obliged us. We then heard her making a nest from 6.15 to 6.30 pm and then it was quiet. We wanted to be sure that she was settled, so we stayed until it was very dark at 7.00 pm. There was only the occasional noise from the canopy, which sounded like Temara adjusting her position in her nest to get comfortable.

We trekked back to the station and I felt a great sense of relief, as Temara had now been in the jungle for two days and I thought that, all things considered, it was going extremely well. I was starving and scoffed down a big dinner. Despite being exhausted when we got back to the vet clinic that night, I managed to send the following email update to everyone back home, since I knew they were all eagerly awaiting news of how Temara's first days in the forest had unfolded.

Hi everyone,

I'm just sending a really quick email as I have to get to bed because I'm so tired. It's Temara's second day in the jungle and we spent 14 hours in the forest today. We got up at 4.30 am and left the jungle at 6.55 pm. Good Lord I'm exhausted. Have to get up same time tomorrow so have just had a quick dinner and a mandi and then off to sleep for me. That's if I can sleep – I think I have gone past being able to sleep.

Quick summary:

1. Temara is a legend.
2. Temara slept in till 12.30 pm today! Why did we have to get to her sleeping site at 5.30 am?
3. Temara travelling quite well in afternoon – crossing between trees beautifully and carefully except when she did her daredevil swing from one tree to another 8 metres away by a vine that was about 8 mm thick (or should I say thin?).
4. Has come down to ground occasionally but much better than yesterday.
5. Has hand-fed from me and Leif so that's great as she can get extra food when she needs.
6. Has often been about 30 metres up in tree. Fantastic but God my neck hurts!!!
7. Has been trying numerous forest fruits.
8. Has thrown things at us (some things never change).
9. Her main drama at the moment is making (or not making) a night nest. She leaves it too late because she's still foraging in the late afternoon and then she suddenly gets agitated and has a tantrum as if to say 'Where the hell am I going to sleep?' This is why we are staying in the forest until 7 pm, because Temara is still fluffing away up in the dark. I was really upset for her last night but she was a bit better tonight and did start to settle a bit earlier so hopefully she'll only improve.

All in all Temara's done very well and it's only Day 2 so we are very proud of her. Even Peter, who is in charge of the release site, has been impressed and he has very high standards.

Well I better go,

Hugs to everyone,
Kylie

Temara during the first week of her release (Photo: Peter Pratje)

10

Nocturnal swamp girl

I started to find my feet after a few days of following Temara in the jungle. My feet just happened to be submerged in a leech-infested swamp. Temara had quickly developed into what I called the 'nocturnal swamp orangutan', and had taken up residence in the canopy above a swamp. This meant that every morning at 5.20 am and every evening at 6.45 pm, all of Temara's trackers had to traipse through a 20-metre swamp with spiky rotan everywhere and places where you would sink up to your knees in the mud. Temara seemed quite amused as she watched us from her high and dry vantage point. She would sit about 12 metres up a tree and have the odd nibble on a leaf or twig. Now, I wouldn't have minded so much being in the swamp if she had been eating some fruit, but no, it was just a leaf.

I was taking notes on Temara's activities while holding my backpack and balancing on a large tree root so I wouldn't fall in the swamp. I felt as if I was in the final immunity challenge on *Survivor*. This is usually an endurance challenge, which involves staying in the same position while balanced over something precarious. Except, unfortunately, there was no host named Jeff to offer me my favourite food as an incentive to step out of the challenge. After about thirty minutes, I started to coax Temara out of the swamp with some treats, as there were no good fruit trees for her in this part of the swamp anyway. It took a good while, but after forty-five minutes Temara finally came over to me and then we shooed her up a huge fruit tree where she ate the wild fruit for twenty minutes.

Bees made their presence well known during the first week of Temara's release. On the third day, a swarm of bees surrounded Temara and she became highly agitated as she swatted at them and tried to hide her face. When this strategy didn't work, Temara descended her tree and started running along the ground to escape the angry swarm. The two trackers and I raced after her and she deftly crossed a large swampy area of forest with the trackers following closely behind. I managed to get stuck in the swamp when I was only halfway across. I was knee-deep in mud and there was nothing to grab hold of to pull myself out except spiky rotan branches. As I stood there trying to figure out a solution, the situation became worse when a lone bee landed on the bridge of my nose. I couldn't swat it away since I had my backpack in one hand and my notepad in the other. I desperately started blowing air towards my nose to try to blow the menacing bee off. The bee's response to my desperate blowing was to promptly sting me on the nose. I somehow managed to drag myself out of the heavy mud while cursing the pain-inflicting bee. I found Temara and the trackers after a few minutes and all of us sat there feeling sorry for ourselves, since they had also been stung.

Temara also showed signs of being what David Attenborough might refer to as an 'intriguing nocturnal orangutan subspecies'. Scientific papers written on wild orangutan behaviour state that orangutans generally wake up and start travelling between 6.00 and 8.00 am and make a night nest between 4.30 and 5.30 pm. Well, Temara obviously had not read those papers. She was more of a 'university student orangutan', which involved staying up really late at night and then not bothering to get out of bed until after lunch. One day she didn't leave her nest until 2.30 pm, and I had to lament the fact that I had got up yet again at 4.30 am just in case Temara moved out of her nest at a respectable time. Temara tended to do her best foraging when other orangutans were getting ready to go to sleep, but she soon perfected the art

Recording Temara's evening activities by the light of my head torch

of making a great sleeping nest in the semi-dark when she had finished feeding. Temara was also nesting high up in the canopy. This was a fantastic development, even though it meant a very sore neck for me from constantly looking up into the trees.

I was hoping Temara would start to adjust to a more normal jungle orangutan routine soon, but she had always been a late riser at Perth Zoo, so I wasn't too worried. During the first week, Temara was in a part of the forest that didn't have a great canopy, so she would sometimes go onto the ground to travel quickly to other trees she couldn't reach. We allowed her to do this, but if she sat on the ground for any length of time we would encourage her up a tree. We were quite strict with Temara when it came to coming to the ground in the late afternoon, though. If she showed any signs of descending an appropriate nesting tree after 4.30 pm, we would yell at her to *naik*, or climb. The Indonesian boys would yell *naik* in an annoying, loud nasal tone, and for some reason, my voice also changed to mimic this annoying tone when I yelled out *naik*. It's no wonder this method was so effective in sending Temara bolting back up into the canopy!

On the fifth day of her release, Temara proved to us that there was some hope for her adjusting to an earlier bedtime routine. This occurred at 5.50 pm, when she actually made a nest in a fantastic tree without ever thinking about coming down to the ground. Temara also took the supplementary food from Herman and Perizal, and she seemed much more relaxed with them, so that was another very positive development.

Near the end of the first week of Temara's release, she managed to come across the large cage complex at the release site, which housed twelve young orangutans in release training. A subadult male orangutan was also in the cage. Well, Leif and I wanted none of that! We did not want Temara to get pregnant this early after her release, as we thought it would be best if she had more time to adjust to her new forest life first. This male orangutan had other ideas, and obviously wanted his genes to carry on in BTP. He was staring at Temara while hanging on the mesh, and made a pathetic attempt at a long call to try to impress her. Adult male orangutans will long-call to attract females into their area for mating, and it also warns other males to stay out of their territory. At Perth Zoo, Temara's father, Hsing Hsing, long-calls quite regularly. Rather than long-calling at other threatening orangutan males he would encounter in the jungle, Hsing directs his long calls at more metropolitan species, such as the garbage trucks and other vehicles that amble past his exhibit. Hsing makes it quite clear to the offending noisy vehicles that they are in his territory, and since they always move away from his exhibit while he is in the process of long-calling, I'm sure Hsing has a highly inflated opinion of how tough and scary he really is. Temara was intrigued by this male in the cage, and she watched him with some interest. A more frivolous reason I didn't want Temara to mate with this particular male was that he was really quite ugly. Despite this having no scientific bearing on Temara's success, I did not want her to have an ugly baby!

Temara proceeded to climb onto the roof of the large cage. Some of the young orangutans took a great interest in Temara. It's more than likely that they saw her as a mother figure, since they had all lost their own mothers. Some of the littlest orangutans stretched their arms out of the cage and reached out to Temara as if to say, 'Will you be my mummy?' Temara paused, turned her head to look at them and then reached out her arm towards their hands. I was taken aback by this surprisingly gentle gesture on Temara's part, but the real Temara soon shone through as she then proceeded to swat their little hands away. I shook my head at Temara and felt bad for the orphaned little mites that had just wanted some motherly affection. I managed to coax Temara about 30 metres away from the cage, and she made her nest in a large tree. I had a bad feeling that she would be reluctant to move away from the very interesting cage area. My suspicions were soon proven correct.

Temara stayed at the cage for another three long days. I tried to move her away from the area so she would begin to travel and forage again of her own accord but she had other ideas. She was being so stubborn and she knew how to push my buttons. Despite my frustration, I would put on my happy face and sweet orangutan-bribing voice in my quest to coax her away from the cage. I showed her a plethora of treats I would give her if she

Temara looking down at the big cage from her high vantage point (Photo: Peter Pratje)

followed me. Her response was to sit on a branch near the cage, look at me and chew on the rubber rope that led from the large cage to her tree. Her expression clearly stated, 'Why would I want your stupid food when I can chew on rubber just to spite you?' My only response was a silent 'Grrrrrrrr', since I didn't want Temara to know she was clearly winning this battle of wills.

Leif left the release site and headed back to Perth after Temara had been in the jungle for nine days. The plan had always been for him to leave once we felt comfortable with Temara's initial progress in the jungle. The weight on my shoulders was palpable, as I now felt solely responsible for Temara's adaptation to living in the jungle. Leif's parting words to me were both inspiring and daunting: 'I wouldn't trust Temara to anyone else'. I didn't sleep a wink that night.

I had no choice but to gather my composure the next day. I developed the mantra 'I can do this' as I faced another two months in the jungle with Temara, bees, leeches and soggy feet. Unfortunately, Temara was heading for a very average grade for the second week of her release, due to her constant laziness and stubbornness. After three days in a row of not getting out of bed earlier than 1.00 pm, not foraging well and not moving away from the large cage, she did some overnight cramming and scored an A+ on Day 14. This brought relief and satisfaction to me, as I do not like bad report cards for myself or for my students! Only As will do.

Temara's day began at 9.26 am. Yes, that's right, Temara woke up in the morning and started travelling immediately. She found numerous fruits and wild banana leaves during the day. She even ate – or should I say devoured? – some honeycomb from a beehive that she found on the ground. Temara also came across her first ever river. She was intrigued and very curious. She crossed over the river using overhead vines and then climbed down low so she could scoop water out of the river to drink. We were all impressed when she undertook this totally wild orangutan behaviour, and she looked like she had been doing it all her life. Temara finished off her perfect day by making a fabulous sleeping nest at 5.45 pm and was settled by 6.00 pm. I think she had exhausted herself after such an active day. I was excited because we were able to head back to the station for dinner twenty minutes earlier than normal.

Later in the week we were confronted with our arch nemesis – bees. They were everywhere, and despite loving all animals, I was really beginning to develop a grudge against the constant swarms of bees chasing us. If Temara got stung, she would bolt to the ground and run away with the bees and us following her. The bees were very prevalent this particular month, and other released orangutans were also getting chased and stung. Bees were definitely on the cons list of jungle living. When Temara ran to escape the bees, she often travelled through very rough terrain, so it was difficult to keep up with her. Temara's trackers and I would split up when we followed her, to try to cut her off on either side. Herman and Perizal would move with ease and poise though the jungle without making a sound or getting hurt in any way. My performance included the sounds of crashing, branches being snapped, clothes ripping and profanities ringing in the jungle air as I was chased by bees and stabbed by rotan spikes.

Despite Temara having attitude and being very independent, there were moments in the jungle when she showed she had complete faith and trust in me. One day after she had been chased by bees, we were in a poor area of forest with little fruit. We began to lead Temara to a better forest area about 600 metres away. Temara followed me along the winding path and let me check her face and head for bee stings. At one point she even held my hand gently...and then stabbed me with her thumbnail. Gee thanks, Temara! At least I knew she was okay.

While bees took out first place on my 'Cons of Jungle Living' list, rain came in second. I actually became quite religious while living in the jungle, and would chant phrases such as 'Please, God, don't let it rain. Please, God, don't let Temara get attacked by bees. Please, God, don't let Temara go into that swamp area, and again, please don't let it rain!' Of course I knew how important rain was; I just wished it would rain at night and not while I was out doing observations. It would also be better for Temara if it rained at night while she was huddled up safely in her deluxe night-nest chateau (hopefully with a rain roof) rather than during the day, as the rain would reduce her travelling and foraging time.

I didn't mind so much if it only started to rain in the afternoon, since the end of the day was in sight, but to get out of bed in the pitch black at 4.30 am with it raining was really quite depressing. There are not many things more unpleasant than being saturated for fourteen hours. It didn't matter how much wet-weather gear I had on, after a big downpour I would be soaked through and smell like a mouldy, wet rag. It was also very difficult to keep Temara in view when it was raining, because she would hide in the canopy to keep dry. Raindrops would intermittently land in my eyes and temporarily blind me when I looked up into the canopy.

Another hazard of following an orangutan in the rain is trying to travel quickly through the jungle while wearing wet-weather gear. Leif left me his large waterproof poncho, despite the fact that I used to constantly laugh at him wearing it. I soon stopped laughing, though, since Leif would always remain a lot drier than me. Now this poncho was absolutely huge on me, and reached the ground since I am so short. If I was wearing the giant poncho and Temara started moving quickly, I had to scoop it up like a wedding dress, run after her and hope I didn't fall over and die. I would hate to have been identified in a morgue wearing a smelly, hugely oversized poncho!

During the second week of Temara's release, I had to decide how much supplementary food to give her. I didn't want to give her too much extra food in case she became lazy and didn't search for her own forest food, but I didn't want to give her too little, since she needed nutrients and energy to help her adapt to such new living conditions. I thought it was best to err on the side of caution so early after she had been released. After discussing Temara's nutritional requirements via email with Simone, the senior vet at Perth Zoo, we decided that Temara would still be able to enjoy some remnants of her life at Perth Zoo, and that was a decent feed in the evening before she made her nest to settle down for the night.

11

Attack of the angry bees

Up until and including Day 19 of Temara's release, things had been going quite smoothly. Week 3 seemed to be a time of consolidation in which Temara built on her jungle skills. These included travelling, foraging, interacting with other orangutans, and becoming familiar with her surroundings. My major concern at this time was that Temara seemed to be quite fussy with some of the forest fruits, even with types that all the other orangutans ate readily. Temara wouldn't stay in any one fruit tree for any length of time. She would browse for a few minutes and eat a few fruits but would then move on as if looking for something better. I did various things to try to combat this, including eating the fruits myself in front of her. I felt like one of those parents trying to convince their suspicious toddler that mashed pumpkin with peas really does taste good. I would put the fruit in my mouth, chew it, make 'Mmm, yummy' noises and then swallow it...despite the fact that it was foul, bitter and made my tongue burn and eyes water. Like most suspicious toddlers, however, she wasn't fooled.

On a more positive note, Temara was travelling more and often started moving away from her nest by mid-morning, which was early for her. Up until Day 20, she had stayed in a relatively small area. She became quite familiar with the area and could easily navigate to certain trees and trails, but then, unfortunately, she made her way back to the large cage after leaving it six days earlier. An adult female orangutan named Putri and her infant son, Paul, were now housed in the cage. Putri was known to be quite aggressive towards other orangutans and also the technicians. Temara decided to assert some authority while visiting the cage, and had a scuffle with Putri through the cage bars. I was actually hoping Putri might give Temara a good nip through the bars, to discourage her from coming onto the cage, but Temara had other ideas. After Temara's second visit to the cage, poor Putri was cowering in the corner of her cage in an effort to hide from the new Queen of BTP – Temara! Herman and I had to yell at Temara to climb the large tree near the cage when she was showing aggression towards Putri. Temara moved away from Putri's cage and onto the tin roof of the cage complex. She did not appreciate being yelled at, and she banged her fist on the tin roof in retaliation. She then proceeded to try to rip the tin sheeting off the roof. Peter happened to be nearby at the time, and he jokingly threatened to invoice Perth Zoo for the damage if she succeeded. I just smirked and looked the other way.

Temara had some very late nights during Week 3, and she was often building night nests after 7.00 pm. I was getting a bit agitated at her because of the risk of us losing sight of her in the dark. I was normally also starving by this stage and just wanted to have some dinner and go to bed! I think Temara's late nights were mainly due to the fact that the sky was quite light because of a full moon. For two nights in a row, Perizal and I had to be very strict with her and yell *naik* when it looked like she was thinking of going to the ground to go to a new tree. At one point we had to bang on the tree she was in and shake vines. Well, two can play at that game. Temara broke off a loose tree branch and threw it at Perizal and then raced down the vine to wallop me on the back. Darling orangutan she is! Perizal and I couldn't help but have a giggle at Temara's tantrum. She finally settled in a nest at 7.20 pm, and Perizal and I could then make the journey back to the station by the light of our head torches.

I'm glad I didn't know what Day 20 of Temara's release had in store for us when I went to bed the night before, otherwise I probably would have had a nervous breakdown and would not have slept a wink. I was expecting it to be quite a boring day, because Temara had slept in the huge tree next to the cage complex and I thought she might not even leave that area at all. In hindsight, that was wishful thinking. In the early afternoon, Temara did what I had been dreading she would do – bolt! This was due to another bee attack, but this wasn't just any swarm of bees. It was a massive swarm and they were angry!

Temara was badly attacked. I could see the bees swarming all around her head and I saw her body flinch every time she was stung. She was extremely agitated. She hit and swatted at the bees but nothing helped, so she ran. Unfortunately, she headed north towards a huge ravine we did not want her to cross. Perizal and I raced after her and managed to get ahead of her in an effort to block her from going into the ravine. We knew that if she went in there we would surely lose her, and I was desperate for that not to happen. But there isn't much you can do to stop a stressed and angry orangutan from moving in the direction it wants to go, and despite my last-ditch effort of throwing myself in front of Temara 5 metres in front of the ravine, she deftly manoeuvred past me and began her descent.

Perizal steadied himself at the top of the ravine to assess his options and then began his descent in pursuit of Temara, using saplings as support. Without thinking I blindly followed him, as I did not want to lose Temara. For that matter, neither did I want to lose Perizal, as I didn't really have any idea where we were. By this stage Temara must have managed to escape some of the bees, and so they turned on Perizal and me. It was a vicious attack, and each of us received more than twenty stings on our head, neck and face. The bees were relentless, and I literally had to grab hold of their bodies and pull them out of my quickly swelling face. Perizal made it to the bottom of the ravine and dived into the river to escape the bees. I was still 30 metres behind him, and like a desperate child lost and terrified in a supermarket, I began to cry. I couldn't help it. I was in agony from all of the stings, I couldn't keep up with Perizal and worst of all there was no sign of Temara.

I basically slid down the rest of the ravine to the river on my arse, since I thought that was the quickest way down. I desperately dived under water as well but managed to keep my backpack above the water, as I didn't want all of my precious observation notes on Temara to be ruined. I staggered to my feet and through tears and sweat yelled for Temara. There was no sign of her. Perizal was scanning the opposite side of the ravine and suddenly we both saw a flash of orange hair. Thank God, it was Temara! While Perizal and I were making our ungracious descent down the ravine, Temara had already managed to scale the other side. Perizal was after her in an instant, but we had a lot of ground to make up. My legs felt like jelly, but they somehow started running again in a bid to catch up with Perizal. I dragged myself up the ravine using saplings and anything else I could grab to help pull myself up the steep ascent.

After the chase had gone on for more than fifteen minutes, I couldn't even see Temara. I was just barely keeping sight of Perizal. I put my trust in him and hoped he wouldn't lose her. Finally, after what seemed like an eternity, Temara stopped running. She collapsed on the ground in exhaustion and Perizal and I followed suit. A few persistent bees still hovered above Temara's head but she didn't react to them. The three of us lay on our backs on the jungle floor for about thirty minutes, chests heaving and our multiple bee stings burning. I was so upset for Temara and I felt pure hatred towards those bastard bees that wouldn't leave her alone. I started to have a bit of a cry, but my face was already starting to swell and it hurt too much to cry, so I just had to suck it up.

I had some fruit and vegetables in my bag for Temara's supplementary feed later that day, so I offered her some as she lay on the ground. I was relieved when she ate quite eagerly. I also gave her half of my water, since she'd had such a strenuous afternoon. By about 4.00 pm Temara had settled down, so Perizal and I started to lead her back to the station area. It seemed to take an eternity, but I think that was just because I was utterly exhausted. Temara was so good and followed me readily along the track. Again, she had shown complete trust in me when she was in a stressful situation. This reaffirmed to me the bond we shared. Luckily, Leif had left me some muesli bars when he returned to Perth, and I happened to have one in my bag that day. This was very useful in leading Temara away from the ravine area. I didn't care that it wasn't on our Perth Zoo orangutan approved diet list! Thankfully, Temara climbed a tree when we were about 60 metres north of the kitchen area. She also ate forest fruit in her nesting tree from 6.00 to 6.40 pm, so that was a great end to a very stressful day.

Perizal and I staggered to the kitchen for dinner at about 7.30 pm. Most of the other boys laughed at us because we were filthy and our faces were already quite swollen from the bee stings. Sukila, the cook, felt sorry for me and decided to help by making me a brown paste-like substance to put on my swollen face. I worked out that she wanted me to put it on my face just before I went to bed, to help ease the swelling. I said thank you, nodded in agreement and then tried not to think about the fact that it looked like a cup of runny dog poop.

After a quick dinner I made my way back to the vet clinic and looked forward to going to bed. I knew, however, that I had to tell Leif what had happened and that it would take too long over email, so I decided to use the satellite phone. It probably cost about $24 a minute to use, but this was an emergency. As soon as Leif answered, I just burst into tears. I was surprised he didn't think it was a crank call and hang up on me. I managed to blubber through the story of the day from hell. Leif is one of the most calm and logical people I know, so it was good to talk the situation through with him and agree on some outcomes. Leif gave me advice and some sympathy, which I gratefully accepted while trying to contain my irregular and uncontrollable sobs. Leif suggested that I needed to take a few days off to recuperate but I said no to this because I didn't want to leave Temara after such a stressful event. He also said I should call the SOS medical emergency number to get some advice on my allergic reaction to the bee stings, and I agreed to do this in the morning. And with that I had a *mandi*, hopped into my pyjamas, put the brown dog-poo-like paste on my face and fell into bed half-unconscious.

I woke up at about midnight with an extremely high temperature and my skin felt like it was on fire. I had developed a new all-over body rash that I technically described as 'dark red and splotchy'. There was not one part of my body that wasn't covered in this bee-sting-induced rash. I barely slept, but I didn't really care because I was worried I might die in my sleep from the allergic reaction I was having to the stings. I must have finally drifted off, though, because when I woke up again at 5.00 am, I thought I had gone blind because I couldn't see when I opened my eyes. Well that wasn't technically true; I couldn't actually open my eyes at all due to the extreme swelling. After I rubbed at them a bit I could see through a slit in my left eyelid, but my right eye was swollen completely shut.

I had no idea what I looked like, since I didn't have a mirror. So I held my camera out in front of me and took a photo of my face and looked at that. I didn't know whether to laugh or cry. I looked absolutely appalling. In fact, it didn't look like me at all. I looked like I had gone ten rounds in a boxing ring: my nose was fat and swollen; my eyes looked like big swollen tennis balls; and the soft delicate skin under my eyes was so filled with fluid that I could jiggle it around. Now that was quite disgusting. I emailed my friends and family that night and told them about the bee chase. I toned the story down in my email to Mum. I also only sent the photo of my hideous face to my friends, and made them swear they would never let my mum see it, because I knew she would be horrified and want me to come home. I only showed Mum the photo once I returned home, but it turned out my suspicions were correct.

I still somehow managed to make it back into the jungle to follow Temara the day after the bee stings. I knew where she was located, so I didn't go out there until about 8.00 am. Poor Perizal had been there since 5.30 am, and when I arrived we smirked at each other because of how terrible we looked. Temara looked absolutely fine. As the day wore on, though, I began to feel quite

My swollen face two days after the bee attack

sick, so I headed back to camp in the early afternoon to have a rest. Perizal also had another tracker with him that day, so I thought I would be safe having my first few hours off in BTP after five weeks. Well, of course that wasn't to be. Temara was on the move again at 3.00 pm and was travelling quite quickly, so the trackers called me on the two-way radio to come out. I was dreading another exhausting afternoon, but thankfully Temara remained within the trail system and was well east of the ravine. I was relieved.

Because of Temara's new location, we now came out of the forest in the evening near the kitchen. As it was already after 7.00 pm, I didn't want to walk all the way back to the vet clinic, have my *mandi* and then head back up to the kitchen for dinner.

First, I just couldn't be bothered because I was exhausted, and secondly, I was worried that all the good food would be gone. So, my new evening routine consisted of trudging out of the forest and straight to the kitchen to have my dinner. I was sopping wet, filthy, stinky and I had a big, fat swollen face. I'm sure I offended numerous people, since all the boys who work there would roll up to dinner looking like they were starring in a fabulous washing-powder commercial, with their clothes so clean and sparkling, and their hair neat and lovely too. And then there was me, the stinky, dirty, swollen-faced foreign girl. But oh well, I got to eat my potato cakes, corn fritters and favourite vegetables, so I didn't mind being an outcast.

So despite a very rough end to Week 3 of Temara's release, it was brilliant that we didn't lose her and that she had recovered well after the bee attack. I was very relieved yet also realistic. I knew we could lose track of her in certain situations, but I took comfort in the fact that Temara had already shown so many positive signs of being able to live in the jungle. I was still confident that she would survive and succeed, even if she didn't have us watching her every move.

12

Hooray, a flushing toilet

Temara actually spent most of the fourth week of her release without me. I definitely found it harder to be away from her than she did me. That, of course, was a good thing, since I was only going to be at BTP until mid-January 2007. Days 22 and 23 of Temara's release saw her behave more like a wild orangutan. She rose early on both mornings, had a midday rest and had made a night nest by 5.30 pm. Temara's travelling and foraging also increased, which was very positive.

An obvious area of Temara's development was her increase in skill when transferring to new trees. Rather than coming to the ground occasionally to travel to a better tree, Temara started to make better use of vines and smaller trees to travel through gaps in the canopy. Her transfers were also becoming more daring, and I suffered numerous minor heart seizures while watching her. Not a day went by, however, when I didn't marvel at the fact that Temara, a zoo-born orangutan, was now living and travelling through the rainforest canopy in a Sumatran jungle. The sheer amount of stimulation and enrichment that provided was more than the best zoo in the world could ever offer. Temara was free to make endless choices about where to go and what to do during the day.

One of the most interesting things to observe was Temara assessing whether certain vines or fragile branches were strong enough to hold her weight before she undertook a tree transfer in the canopy. Temara would reach out and pull on the potential hanging pathway before releasing her grip from her secure tree. However, like other orangutans, Temara did suffer the odd fall. One rainy afternoon, she was in a small tree, snapping off branches. The next minute, she snapped one too many branches and plummeted 5 metres to the ground. My heart literally stopped, and I stood there frozen, with my eyes half-shut, as if watching a B-grade horror movie. Herman and Perizal cracked up laughing and then Temara's head popped up from behind a shrub. She looked embarrassed more than anything, and quickly ran to the nearest tree and scaled it in a flash. After seeing Temara was fine, I turned around and had a little chuckle myself.

Leif and other zoo managers, including the CEO herself, insisted that after spending more than five weeks in BTP without any time off and enduring the hideous bee attack, I needed a few days off to rest. I was very reluctant to leave Temara, and Leif knew this. Unbeknown to me, he had already emailed Peter to ensure that I was on the next transport out of BTP to spend a few days in a hotel in Jambi City. On the day we left for Jambi, I made the trek out to say a temporary goodbye to Temara. She returned the favour by sleeping for the two hours I was there and not even acknowledging my presence.

The journey to Jambi was an eventful and uncomfortable one. Senna, a young female orangutan, made the journey with us, since she appeared to have liver damage and required tests and X-rays. So that meant the vet, all of the bags, an orangutan in a travel crate and I were all squashed into the back of a closed-in jeep.

Now I thought bees were unpleasant, but this trip didn't prove to be much fun either. The jeep was extremely hot, there were no windows in the back and I began to feel carsick after twenty minutes. I had a terrible track record over the last two years when it came to vomiting on various modes of transport, including planes and boats. I did not want to add a car to my list, especially since I'd just eaten rice and corn fritters for lunch, and I really did not want to see them the second time around! To make matters worse, it felt like I was on a ride at an amusement park, because the car was bouncing around so much due to the extremely rough muddy road. And to top it all off, after thirty minutes, little Senna became 'Stinky Senna', when she did an extremely large and unpleasant-smelling poop.

I was desperately trying to stick my head as close to the driver's window as possible, to breathe in some fresh air and avoid vomiting, which would make the jeep smell even worse. This was difficult in itself, since the bench seat I was sitting on faced towards the middle of the jeep and I was busy trying to prevent all of the precariously balanced bags from bouncing off the top of the orangutan crate and onto my head. After about two hours, when we had passed the worst of the rough terrain, we stopped and 'Stinky Senna' was relegated to the roof so she could get some breeze and, more importantly in my opinion at that stage, I could breathe and move my legs again!

After a quick bathroom stop in the bushes, we were on the road again. I was feeling better in no time and looking forward to the trip, because I find it so interesting looking at all of the local people, the little villages and then the larger towns. I had forgotten, however, how manic Indonesian roads can be! Once we were on the larger roads, they actually had white lines painted on them – including solid 'Do not overtake' lines. They might as well not be there, though, because I don't know how many times we were going around a corner when what appeared to be a Mack truck was heading right for us. It sometimes seemed that the drivers liked to play chicken, and it was a case of who would move out of the way at the last second. Sometimes, others liked to join in the game, including motorbikes, a dog and the odd family of chickens or goats. After a few of these incidents, I decided it was better to view the sights while looking out the back window of the jeep. Ignorance, after all, is bliss!

The driver was once again the Mr Miyagi lookalike, so he provided some comic relief during moments of near death! If we had a close call and he heard me gasp in horror, he would turn around and look at me, throw his head back, and laugh maniacally as if to say, 'Ahh, that was close, wasn't it?' We also heard the orangutan crate creak and move a few times up on the roof rack. When this happened, we all looked at each other nervously and then looked out the back window to make sure our most precious passenger wasn't bouncing off the roof and into a ditch.

Our journey took longer than expected due to running out of petrol and breaking down at least four times. On one of the stops we were on the side of the road for more than two hours as Mr Miyagi became 'Mr Fixit' and replaced a bolt or a strap or something of that nature under the bonnet. For the next two hours there were some very strange smells and noises coming from the engine, so I just crossed my fingers that the jeep would make the rest of the journey. Finally, at 10.00 pm (nine hours after

The journey out of BTP is always an experience

we had left BTP), I was dropped off at the hotel...the very nice Novotel! There was a wedding going on and there were about eight luxury cars in the driveway. I staggered out of the dirty, smelly jeep, in my equally dirty, smelly clothes and into the huge, pristine and fancy foyer. I made my way up sheepishly to the main desk and already felt the stares from numerous businessmen in their expensive suits, sitting in the lobby and smoking cigars.

I was wearing filthy, three-quarter-length army pants, an orangutan T-shirt, brown thongs – and my hair looked like I had been though a wind tunnel. Plus my pants sat quite low, and I must have lost some weight because it felt as if they were hanging halfway down my butt! I had put a safety pin in, but that had come loose, so I was just praying that my T-shirt was pulled down far enough to cover the fluoro-green undies I may well have been flashing to more than ten businessmen as I checked in at the main desk. I then had the man at the desk ask if I knew what the nightly rate was and add that they would need a credit-card deposit. I think he wondered, 'How can this filthy girl afford to stay here?' I looked at the rate, smiled sweetly and said, 'That's fine' – but only because I knew that Perth Zoo was paying!

It did feel very strange to be in a lovely hotel room with an extremely large and comfortable bed, and not sharing the room with spiders, mosquitoes and things that went bump in the night. It was very hard not to think about Temara the whole time, but I did my best to rejuvenate and relax for the three days by watching bad movies on HBO and enjoying electricity and a flushing toilet. Just the thought of going back to the leeches and swamps gave me the urge to look in the mini-bar again and flick through all the TV stations! I also put some of my stinky jungle clothes in to be washed at the hotel laundry, as I never seemed to be able to get them properly clean at the release station. I'm sure the laundry staff were not impressed with my smelly and feral clothes.

My three days of luxury passed in the blink of an eye, unlike my days in the jungle, each of which would seem like a week. My bites and rashes also had a chance to subside, since I wasn't constantly being bitten and sweating while traipsing through the jungle.

After another long road trip, we arrived back at the release site at midnight. It would have been earlier if we hadn't been stuck behind the usual relentless line of trucks transporting oil palm fruits to factories. It was also raining, and we had to change vehicles halfway through the trip. I just wanted to make it back to the station, since I had an early start with Temara the next day.

Just when I was becoming excited about getting to bed, the vehicle came to a stop outside the small village school about twenty minutes from the release station. I was confused and cranky. Why were we stopping at the school at 11.00 pm? I soon discovered that we had stopped to make a midnight furniture delivery to one of the locals. Little did I know that there was a bookshelf under the tarpaulin on the back of our truck! Silly me had thought it was orangutan food. So at 11.30 pm, in the rain, we unloaded furniture into a house. Because obviously, unlike Harvey Norman, the staff at BTP will deliver 24/7!

The road trip ended on a very positive note, however, because Herman came out when we arrived and told me that Temara was doing well. She was waking up earlier, eating more forest fruit and nesting by 5.00 pm! I thought if Temara did that well while I was away, then perhaps I should check into a five-star resort for a week.

I spent the next day out in the jungle observing Temara, and I thought she looked fantastic. She did seem to think that I should have returned to the jungle bearing gifts, though, because from 4.00 to 5.00 pm she kept climbing down quite low and looking hopefully at my backpack. When I said, 'Tidak. Makan buah hutan!' meaning 'No. Eat forest fruit', she became quite offended, shook some vines and threw a small branch at me. Ahh, it was good to be back in the jungle with my favourite girl!

13

Jungle real estate

Week 5 in the jungle at BTP was successful and quite stress-free. On days 29 and 30 of her release, Temara was still in the same area she had nested in for a few days. She had developed quite a lazy routine, because her nest was close to numerous fruiting trees, including one with medium-sized fruit called *kerdongdon*. Temara's trackers told me the fruit was called this because it makes that noise when it falls on your head, but I didn't know if they were just teasing me. *Kerdongdons* are about the size of a nectarine. For five days Temara basically left her nest, travelled to the fruiting trees, gathered some food and returned to her nest to eat her gathered supplies. She also used the same nest to sleep in for numerous nights in a row and simply added more leaves and branches to it each night. When wild orangutans find a rich food supply, they will often stay in the area for weeks at a time, so this was not an unusual behaviour. In spite of this, I wanted Temara to explore more of the trail system around the station area during the fruiting season. This would enable her to discover numerous food sources and possibly meet other orangutans from whom she could learn.

Therefore, on Day 31 of her release, I decided it was time for Temara to move suburbs. Temara's usual trackers were both on a day off, so an experienced tracker named Marjoni was following her for a few days. Temara made it quite clear that she did not approve of Marjoni at all. If he tried to feed her, she would not come down, shook branches and became very agitated. I couldn't really blame her, since Marjoni made me tense as well. He was very strict and not laid-back like the other boys. I was glad I had Temara for company in the jungle when I had to spend the day with someone who would have suited being an SAS soldier.

Because of Temara's dislike of Marjoni, I had to send him ahead and then I coaxed Temara with food treats about 350 metres west down an old logging road. I then wanted to lure her south, but Temara decided she preferred the real estate in the north-east. Consequently, she ran back the way we came for about 50 metres and then headed north. At first I felt a bit deflated, but it proved a successful afternoon, because Temara fed on numerous new fruits, including two quite large fruits, about the size of a small apple. I wish I had taken my camera with me, because at one point her mouth was so full of the fruits that she could barely chew and it looked like she had lockjaw. Temara also found that these fruits were the perfect-sized missiles to launch at Marjoni when he was looking the other way. Marjoni quickly learnt that Temara had an excellent aim, and I had a secret giggle as he had to duck for cover.

Marjoni's tough-guy image took a dive the next day, when in the middle of a downpour he brought out an umbrella. Yes, an umbrella in the middle of the jungle. Now I've seen trackers use lots of creative ways to stay dry, but never a brightly coloured girly umbrella! Temara was not impressed with this foreign object, but it served a dual purpose for Marjoni, since it protected him from both the rain and Temara's high-speed missiles. When Temara started travelling in the downpour and Marjoni followed with his umbrella, it actually made it very easy for me to keep Marjoni in view, since I just followed the bobbing red umbrella.

Temara stayed in this area from 16 to 20 December. During this time she slept in the Taj Mahal of orangutan nests. It took her more than an hour to construct the nest, and she required numerous rest breaks during this epic build. It honestly looked as if the nest contained half the canopy of the tree. She finished making it when it was relatively dark so I couldn't see it properly. When I returned in the morning and saw how huge and magnificent it was, my next thought was, 'Oh, crap, she'll never move out!' By 19 December she was only 20 metres away from a large river. I didn't want Temara to cross the river, as we were getting close to the boundary of the marked trail system. It would be more difficult to follow her in the rougher terrain outside the trail system. Also, if she kept moving further away from the station, we would have to start sleeping in the jungle overnight. I didn't fancy sleeping on the ground in the possible home range of a Sumatran tiger with only insect repellent for protection.

We tried to lure Temara away from the river, but after coaxing her about 40 metres up a particular trail, she ran back and entered the forest at exactly the right location to return to her large nesting tree. Despite being frustrated that I couldn't lead her to a better location, I was very impressed with her orientation skills, as she seemed to become familiar with an area quite quickly. Once back near her mammoth nest, Temara spent the afternoon climbing into a neighbouring small tree and feeding on a small red fruit called *kapialan*. She would also break small branches off a tree that had fruit on it and then climb back up to her nest so she could eat in bed. I thought this was quite amusing, since most humans greatly enjoy the indulgence of occasionally eating in bed.

I was still evaluating how much supplementary food to give Temara, as it was difficult to assess how much forest fruit she was actually eating high up in the canopy. I emailed our zoo vet Simone again for some advice. After some discussion, we decided I should offer Temara 20 per cent of her daily calorie requirement of 1,900 Calories (7,900 kJ) as supplementary food on a daily basis. Temara received her 380 Calories of supplementary food from a mixture of fruits, gourds, tubers, protein and carbohydrates. I would choose items from these categories depending on what foodstuffs were available, but they mainly included mandarins, bananas, mangoes, cucumber, sweet potato, eggs and rice. I knew that Temara's supplementary feeding regime would be adjusted over time depending on her foraging habits and energy levels. I also planned to introduce one or two days per week when she would not be given any supplementary food, so that she would not always expect free food. I hoped this would give her further incentive to forage for more forest fruits and other food sources throughout the day.

Week 6 observing Temara included Christmas Day in the jungle. Christmas Day started for me when I woke up at 3.49 am. I had to get up at 4.45 am, so I could not get back to sleep. Plus the small wild animal that lived on the roof of our accommodation was extremely active – either that or it was Santa Claus saying, 'Where is the damn chimney and why do I have rice and chilli instead of cookies and milk?'

Christmas breakfast at 5.00 am consisted of rice, noodles and spicy potato wedges. Lunch consisted of leftover rice, noodles and spicy potato wedges. But it was alfresco dining under Temara's nesting tree, so that was nice. Well actually, it wasn't that nice, since the only available space to sit down included Temara's designated toilet area.

I had not been getting much sleep, and when I'm overtired I behave as if I've had a few too many wines, so I think I kept everyone entertained. First of all, Herman kept falling asleep so I kept putting leaves all over him and taking photos. Perizal thought this was hilarious and tried to muffle his laughter by covering his mouth. Once Herman woke up, he was in fine form and sang numerous songs to Temara. Then I thought it was time to dance the limbo, but no one else wanted to play, so Sabine and a palm tree had to hold the limbo stick while I limboed away. At least I had fun.

Sabine and I also wrote a Sumatran jungle Christmas carol called 'Jungle Bells' that should be sung to the tune of 'Jingle Bells' – I really think it could be a hit:

Jungle Bells

Dashing through the jungle
In leech-proof socks and shoes
Sitting, watching Temara
Something smells like poo!

Trying to lure her south
It's proving quite a test
Temara says, 'It's Christmas,
I'm going back to my nest!'

It's time for Christmas lunch
Oh no, it's noodles and rice

I wish I was back home
So I could have something nice

Dreaming of food back home
Temara's being so boring
She hasn't moved for two hours
So Herman's started snoring

Covering him with leaves
Perizal's trying not to laugh
Taking a quick photo
Then nicking off down the path

Sabine and Kylie finish early
Because it's Christmas Day
Going down the Trampelpfad★
Slipping and sliding all the way

Made it back to the kitchen
Took off our stinky things
Sitting there and waiting
For presents Santa didn't bring

We go back to our house
To our homemade Christmas tree
Christmas was still fun in the jungle
Especially since there were no bees.

★*Trampelpfad*: German for small, narrow path. We're very multicultural here at BTP!

Sabine and I made a fantastic Christmas tree out of a fallen tree branch. We hung handmade paper decorations and jungle fruits on it. I placed the tree in a bucket and put it against a trusty blue Qantas blanket hung up on the wall, so it looked very festive! The only problem was that it made me jump with fright every time I got up during the night to go to the toilet.

Our indoor jungle Christmas tree

At 3.00 pm on Christmas Day, Sabine and I went back to the kitchen and had a lovely surprise waiting for us. The office crew in Jambi had sent us a Christmas hamper with Coke and various biscuits. By 8.00 pm I'd drunk strong coffee and Coke and had chocolate cookies (well, I think it was chocolate-flavoured cardboard), so I lay in bed awake for most of the night.

Like most people back home in Australia, who were probably spending the Christmas period lazing about and eating too much food while watching the cricket, Temara also seemed to enjoy the holiday season by relaxing and not doing much at all. She had been in the same area for more than a week and was very reluctant to move. My boredom at watching her doing nothing soon evaporated when the adult female Putri and her son Paul from the large cage, made an appearance. They had been released a few days earlier and they were now in very close proximity to Temara's nesting tree. I did not want Temara and Putri to come into contact, since they would probably have a nasty fight, so I was instantly on high alert.

Putri's trackers made every effort to move Putri and Paul to a different location, but they were very scared of Putri because she would often come to the ground and chase them. At one point Putri came quite close to Perizal and me. Perizal squealed like a five-year-old girl, grabbed my hand and dragged me about 50 metres up the path to escape Putri's wrath. I couldn't help but smirk, since Putri made Temara look friendly! One of the funniest scenes I remember from this BTP trip involved Putri and her two trackers. They had to be strict with her, since she kept travelling on the ground and this is very dangerous for orangutans, as they can become prey to Sumatran tigers. Perizal and I were sitting quietly, waiting for Temara to wake up, when suddenly Putri came running up the hill carrying Paul as her two trackers chased her and waved sticks to encourage her to climb. They disappeared up the hill and then all was quiet. Two minutes later, the tables had turned and the two trackers came sprinting back down the hill, this time with an angry Putri in pursuit. Temara's laziness finally paid off, because she was still sleeping in her nest while this commotion took place below her. Thankfully, after much bribing from her trackers, Putri moved away from the area and I breathed a sigh of relief.

Temara was still close to the river we didn't want her to cross. We also didn't want her to move too far west, as that was close to a deep ravine. If Temara crossed this ravine it would mean we could no longer follow her. Being so early into her release, we hoped she would stay within the trail system, so she could be closely monitored. Moving south was our preferred option. Despite numerous attempts to coax Temara in this direction, she would continually turn back and return to her nesting tree. This was frustrating, as we wanted her in a different area, but it was also positive that she chose not to follow me or her trackers for delicious food treats such as corn and eggs. Instead, she would feed on wild fruits, including liana, *tapus* and *kapialan*, in close proximity to her nesting tree. I thought this indicated that she was not overly hungry, despite the fact that she had lost some weight. It also highlighted that she was a strong-willed orangutan and would not move to a new area unless she desired to do so.

One afternoon, I decided to be quite strict with Temara's supplementary food. I explained to Herman that if she didn't follow us to a new location between 3.00 and 4.30 pm to receive her extra food, we wouldn't give it to her. After Temara threw numerous tantrums at us, Herman came up with the mantra, '*Tidak jalan, tidak makan!*' which literally means, 'Don't move, don't eat!' Temara chose to ignore the warning and went and found her own food. Temara's defiance and independence constantly indicated to me that she had every chance of successfully surviving in the jungle on her own.

Despite the fact that Temara did not travel much in Week 6, there were still some very interesting behaviours to observe. She was nesting in a tree that was surrounded by thick undergrowth and swamp. The trackers and I were forced to sit in a tiny area about 20 metres away from Temara's nest because it was the only spot not covered in rotan and infested with leeches. Temara could see the predicament that we were in and, being the thoughtful orangutan she is, decided to make this her new toilet area. She would leave her nest, make her way through the canopy to above where we all sat precariously on a large tree root and then proceed to urinate and defecate. After two days, we couldn't bear the smell any longer, so we created a new little sitting area by clearing some vegetation with a machete. On the plus side, it was easy to record if Temara had defecated, and it was also simple to collect a faecal sample for parasite screenings.

Temara also became extremely entertaining when it came to her nest building. She seemed to outdo herself every week in constructing a huge and impressive nest high in the canopy. Her current nest was massive, but she would add more leaves and branches to it every day so it would be freshly lined. It was quite a wet week, and Temara appeared to collect much of her new nesting material from the canopy beneath her nest, as if to keep the upper canopy more intact for extra rain protection. Temara also occasionally nested in a nearby smaller tree right next to our observation point.

On Christmas Eve, Temara had taken about half the nesting material from her smaller nest and carried it back to the larger nesting tree about 20 metres away while breaking off more branches along the way. By the time she arrived back at her large nest, she was carrying about 24 kilograms of branches on her shoulder through the canopy to add to her large nest. Strangely, in the early evening, Temara then took most of this new nesting material back to the smaller nest and slept there for the night. After that, she travelled between the two nests during the day, often transporting nesting material with her from tree to tree. This was very amusing to watch, and Herman and Perizal even called other trackers over the two-way radio to come and watch Temara's fascinating behaviour. We all had a good laugh as we watched Temara 'move house'.

Temara's gigantic nest

By this time I had also observed the development of a healthy respect between Temara and her two main trackers, Herman and Perizal. They did think Temara could be lazy, but I could tell that they were also impressed with many of the things she had achieved in such a short time. I felt like a proud mum when they said 'Bagus, Temara, bagus', which means 'Excellent' in Indonesian. The trackers would often compare the orangutans they were monitoring and what progress they had made in the jungle. I heard them comment that Putri was spending too much time on the ground and not making a proper night nest. I would shake my head in disappointment and then say how fabulous Temara was because she never came to the ground and made massive night nests high in the canopy. I couldn't help but be competitive. I was soon put back in my place, though, because Putri's trackers would laugh at the fact that Temara had not moved away from 'Trail Z 100' for more than a week.

Temara was a lot more relaxed around Herman and Perizal. This pleased me, because I needed to know that she trusted them before I headed back home in a few weeks' time. They might need to coax Temara into a better area or check her physically for any signs of illness or injury. Despite having more trust in her trackers, she would still ignore them for the majority of the day, and travel and forage of her own accord. This was exactly the balance we wanted.

Another positive event that occurred in Week 6 was Temara's change in bedtime. Rather than fluffing about up in the canopy until after dark, Temara had usually settled for the night in her penthouse nest by 5.30 pm. It was still quite light at this time, so we stayed in the jungle until 6.30 pm, just in case she decided to do some evening exploring. The highlight of Week 6, though, was definitely the disappearance of the dreaded bees. The wet weather had set in and this had seen the demise of our flying arch-enemy. Temara had not been attacked by bees in about two weeks, so her stress levels – and mine – had fallen significantly.

Week 6 ended on 27 December 2006 with Temara finally moving away from her nesting site of the past week at 4.00 pm. Of course she didn't choose a reasonable time to begin her travels, such as 7.00 am or even 1.00 pm – no, of course not, it was 4.00 pm. Temara always seemed to do something exciting and adventurous when most other orangutans were preparing to go to sleep. She moved north and made a night nest about 10 metres away from the river. She ate numerous new fruits while travelling, so that was very positive. It appeared that Week 7 in the jungle could be wet and exhausting, as the area on the north side of the river was very rough and hilly. This was called Bukit Tigapuluh (Thirty Hills) for good reason!

14

A rainy new year

Another week of observing Temara went by at BTP. Her progress continued as she developed new skills. Week 7 proved a rather social week for her, as numerous orangutans moved through the area she had stayed in for the past week. Temara actually behaved herself very well and didn't show aggression towards any of the other orangutans. I was quite relieved about this. She definitely appeared to be dominant over all the orangutans she encountered, though. This was not surprising, considering her strong personality as well as her large size compared to most of the other released orangutans at BTP. I was still concerned that Putri and Temara remained in close proximity, because there was a high chance of aggression between these two adult females, but Putri mainly travelled on the ground, and we hoped she would move away from Temara's area in the near future.

Temara again developed a deliberate and comfortable routine in her new nesting area, just south of a river within the mapped trail system. She slept in a lot during the week, but there were some fruiting trees near her two nesting trees, so she had plenty of food to eat once she started travelling. The main foods she ate in this area were *angal, tapus, lepang kayu* and *panto* fruits. In each location, she continued to eat liana stem, leaves and fruit, as liana is very common in the jungle. As in the previous week, the new area Temara utilised was quite small, and she even had a set route she followed while foraging. I could sometimes even follow my own footprints as I tracked her. I did not try to lure her away from this area, however, because she was foraging well and had shown she was smart enough to travel to a new area once the fruit sources had been utilised or she had become bored.

Whenever I was sitting still in the forest, I became acutely aware of any nearby noise, including debris falling from the canopy. I was very wary of the risk of being knocked unconscious by a plethora of organic material falling from the sky. This falling debris was usually caused by an orangutan moving through the canopy, and could be easily avoided by maintaining a respectful distance from the orangutan. There were also times, however, when half the tree canopy seemed to malfunction and come crashing to the ground for no apparent reason.

New Year's Eve saw a change in routine for me as Martina, the other main orangutan keeper at Perth Zoo, arrived at BTP. Martina was funded by TOP to conduct a site visit, as TOP financially supported this release site and the Wildlife Protection Units. Marty was also going to spend some time observing Temara with me. I was so excited to have one of my best friends visit me in the depths of the Sumatran jungle. And she came bearing gifts, including mini bottles of champagne, cards with soppy messages in them from my workmates, an eye mask, lollies and cheese. Yes, that's right, cheese, one of my very favourite things in the world. I actually couldn't think of a better New Year's than sitting there gossiping with a great friend and eating cheese, even if it was the triangular plastic-like cheese that doesn't need refrigerating.

Other items in Marty's rather large goody bag included beekeeper hats. One of the Perth Zoo directors had ordered them for Martina to bring up, as she was so horrified at seeing photos of my badly swollen face from the bee stings. The beekeeper hats were bulky and highly unattractive, but we put them on and had a good laugh while Sabine took photos of us posing in them.

As it was New Year's Eve, as a special treat, the generator was left on until 12.30 am, so we stayed up well past midnight chatting and catching up on all the gossip. Marty had a lot more to talk about than me, because I had spent the last eight weeks of my life staring into trees waiting for an orangutan to wake up and move.

Martina also brought me drugs – not the illicit type, just an antihistamine called Phenergan that can also be used as a sleep aid since it can make people drowsy. Everyone back home knew from my emails that I had not been sleeping well at all since we had released Temara. Despite being physically exhausted after spending long days in the jungle, I just couldn't switch my over-thinking brain off at night. I have always done my best thinking at night when most normal people are falling asleep. I would also worry when I went to bed about the upcoming day if I had something stressful on. Considering every day in the jungle proved stressful, I wasn't getting much sleep at all, and I was starting to look like the living dead. I was excited about my new potential sleeping assistant, but it wasn't to be, since my body somehow seemed to be immune to the drowsiness effect.

Temara obviously had a good sleep on New Year's Eve, because she left her nest at 5.40 am on New Year's Day – the earliest time she had ever risen in the morning. Was Temara's New Year's resolution not to be a lazy blob? Unfortunately, I wasn't there to observe this great phenomenon. Martina and I only had about three hours' sleep, so we didn't go into the jungle until 9.00 am. Martina greatly enjoyed the walk up the 550-metre steep incline, followed by the 400-metre flat stretch with prickly ferns surrounding the path and then finally, just for some variety, a 120-metre steep and slippery decline to get to Temara's nesting site. My suggestion to her to not wear any socks on the walk to Temara, to save them from getting saturated and stinky, perhaps wasn't the best idea, since she ended up with a huge blister from her boots instead.

When we arrived at the site, Temara had returned to her nest after her obviously exhausting early start to the day. Martina felt special because when she called out to Temara under her nesting tree, she actually peered down at us from the edge of her nest. She even started to descend the tree quite quickly when Martina offered her a banana. However, not throwing unnecessary tantrums was obviously not one of Temara's New Year's resolutions. Maybe Temara thought that having two Perth zookeepers following her in the Sumatran rainforest was just a bit too suspicious, as she proceeded to shake some vines in disgust and travel in the opposite direction to the proffered banana. We had to have a chuckle at that one.

Martina was quickly impressed by Temara's skills in the forest and thought she was in great physical condition, despite having lost some weight. It was reassuring to get Martina's opinion about Temara's appearance, because she hadn't seen her for two months. It can sometimes be difficult to assess subtle physical changes in an animal or person when you see them every day.

New Year's Day started out with the first blue sky in more than a week, but by the early afternoon the rain was coming down in buckets. The boys had set up a great rain shelter a few days earlier using branches and sheets of tin (don't ask me how you come across tin in the middle of the jungle), but it had been knocked over by a rogue orangutan the day before. We put our jungle survival skills to the test and hastily re-erected the shelter using vines to secure and connect different pieces. Martina, Sabine and I then all huddled under the little shack.

Alas, our makeshift shelter didn't last long. We hadn't realised how many small holes were in the metal sheeting until we started getting wet. I volunteered to save the day by bringing out the huge smelly poncho to drape over the metal sheeting to cover all of the holes. Once out of the shelter I was soaked in about 0.7 seconds. As I flung the poncho lightly over the sheets of tin as you would a sheet on a bed, the entire construction collapsed and the metal sheeting fell on Martina and Sabine's heads. With their screams and me swapping between fits of laughter and saying 'I'm sorry', it must have been a sight to see. So for twenty minutes we sat there, balancing large sheets of rusty, holey metal above our heads in the pouring rain.

Temara was quite active that afternoon and ate numerous forest fruits, so that was great for Martina to see. Martina also experienced the sensation of wearing wet stinky jungle clothes for five hours. That was a lovely New Year's Day experience for her too. All in all, it was a very memorable New Year's, and I had fake cheese to look forward to back at camp, so I was extremely happy.

Overall, Week 7 of Temara's release was very wet. It wasn't so bad if it rained in the afternoon, but if there was a downpour in the morning then my feet would be pure white and wrinkly by the time I got back to the station in the evening. I was waiting

Smiles and frizzy jungle hair on New Year's Day

for fungus to start growing between my toes. During periods of heavy rain, Temara would usually stay in her nest or take cover under a dense tree canopy, but she would still travel and forage in light rain. After a heavy downpour, she would emerge from her canopy cover looking almost dry but with slightly frizzy hair, while I would emerge after the downpour soaking wet and with extremely frizzy hair. It is not good to have curly hair while living in the humid jungle, as it turns into an uncontrollable and unattractive frizz-fest, so I was just grateful that I didn't have a mirror.

With the constant rain, the bees had well and truly disappeared, and this meant that Temara almost never went to the ground. Most of the time she spent on the ground in the first few weeks after her release had been initiated by bee attacks, so no bees meant a settled and contented Temara high in the canopy. And when Temara was content, I was content. I felt very satisfied with her progress and that she excelled at some facets of jungle life, including not coming to the ground. Numerous ex-pet released orangutans at BTP would often attempt to go to the ground and they had to be encouraged to climb.

I began to reduce the amount of time I spent in the jungle watching Temara, since I would be leaving BTP in mid-January. I wanted her to become accustomed to me not being in the jungle all of the time, so it wouldn't be a sudden change for her when I returned home to Australia. It was a bit sad limiting my time with Temara, as I knew there was so little left, but it had to be done for her benefit. Considering Temara had only recently tried to hit me after I gave her some food, I didn't think she would be terribly upset at all when I left, which of course was a good thing!

More time being spent away from Temara meant that Martina and I could visit the small local school. Martina had brought with her a huge box of T-shirts and school supplies for the children. These had been donated by Perth Zoo. The journey to the school proved rather eventful, as we each rode on the back of a motorbike driven by a technician from the release site. I had never been on the back of a motorbike before, so to do it on the muddy and scary roads leading to the school was a rather terrifying experience. I really did think I was going to die, or at least fall off and break a limb. Not having a helmet didn't help calm my nerves either.

I hung onto the back of the motorbike for dear life and tried not to scream in terror in the technician's ear as we bounced our way through potholes, mud and ditches. Halfway through the 20-minute journey, I actually started to relax a little bit. I tried to enjoy the ride and regard it as yet another new experience far from home. I cursed myself for not wearing a hat, because when we arrived at the school, my already frizzy and humidified hair had taken on a life of its own. I was quite concerned that I might scare the small children with my crazy windswept hair.

Martina and I were excited and a little bit nervous when we entered the school. It was a very old and run-down building. All the children shared the one room and one teacher. About twenty-five children were present, ranging in age from about five to sixteen. They all sat there, eyes wide and mouths open, looking intently at the two strange white girls who had come to visit. I asked Julius, one of the staff at BTP, to translate for me since my Indonesian was still quite basic. I explained to the children that Temara had come from Perth Zoo to live in the Sumatran jungle that was her home and that she loved living near their village. I also asked Julius to explain the importance of the forest ecosystem to the children. As well, he told them that people all over the world love orangutans and that we need their help to protect them. We then gave out the T-shirts and school supplies, and I said they were a gift from Temara and Perth Zoo. It was lovely to see the children open up the gifts so excitedly. I hoped Temara's generosity at gift-giving would make her the most popular orangutan in Sumatra, and that the desire to protect the BTP ecosystem would be high on the children's list of priorities.

Those implementing the orangutan release program at BTP have worked hard to ensure local community involvement and engagement. Local people are employed as technicians at the release site and others are members of the Wildlife Protection Units. An education team is also employed. This team makes regular visits to schools and villages in a vehicle painted with very distinctive tiger stripes. The main aim of the team is to educate the communities about the importance of protecting natural forest habitat. It is crucial that the people in the villages surrounding the BTP ecosystem understand and support this vital release program.

It is very easy for people in First World countries to criticise developing countries like Indonesia for their horrendous rates of both illegal and legal deforestation, but First World countries play a huge role in the demand for products exported from Indonesia at the expense of orangutan habitat. The list of these products is endless, from wooden furniture to a trolley full of groceries laden with palm oil. We are part of the problem and we must be part of the solution.

15

Goodbye, Temara

I had mixed emotions as I observed Temara during my final week in the jungle. I couldn't help but be excited about returning home, but of course I knew I would miss and worry about Temara once I had left. Despite a slow start to Week 8, Temara finally moved away from her comfortable nesting area on 6 January and travelled to a new area on the east side of Trail Z. She fed on numerous new fruits and leaves, and travelled well.

On 7 January, Martina and I arrived at Temara's nesting site at 9.30 am to an unexpected surprise. When I worked with Tatok in BTP in 2005, I also spent a lot of time assisting with forest school lessons for the juvenile orangutans in the cages. My favourite orangutan from forest school was a young male named John Deere, who was about five years old. He wasn't the most attractive orangutan, with a poor coat, a little bald head and a large roll of fat under his chin. But he had a fantastic personality and was very confident in the forest. When he got tired he would go to the ground, put his arms up in the air and make a very distinctive squeaking sound. This squeaking translated to, 'I want cuddles'. One day during forest school, it started pouring with rain and little John Deere sprinted down his tree and plonked himself in my lap and under my raincoat to escape the rain.

John Deere was released in November 2005 and quickly disappeared from the trail system, so was no longer followed. No one had seen him for a year, so when we arrived at Temara's nesting site and I heard the trackers yelling out 'John Deere' I couldn't believe it. When I first saw him I really didn't think it was John Deere. He looked so different, and he had a beautiful long coat. But then he suddenly squeaked and I knew it was him! I excitedly told Martina all about John Deere and how he had blossomed into this beautiful wild orangutan.

Temara soon came out of her nest to observe what all the fuss was about. As soon as John Deere saw Temara, he climbed straight up to visit her. Then five seconds later he came screaming back down the vine with Temara chasing him. I was so annoyed at Temara; why couldn't she ever be nice? Her temper soon abated, though, and then her curiosity took over. Temara and John Deere spent the entire day following each other and interacting at times. They even nested in the same tree and came into contact again on 10 January. I hoped that Temara would spend time observing John Deere, because he had very advanced forest skills, including breaking open termite nests and stripping spiky rotan palms to reach the edible inner stem.

Unfortunately, I waved goodbye to John Deere, as he soon became bored with Temara's lazy morning ways and travelled away from us. From 7 to 10 January, Temara spent most of her time in a *terap* tree and mostly fed on its large fruit, which is about the size of a small mango. This was quite interesting, as Temara would never eat this fruit in the first few weeks after her release. She may have been keener to eat the *terap* fruit now because they were riper and tasted better, but I thought it was probably because she was hungrier and knew that her supplementary feed late in the day would not be enough to satisfy her.

Martina and I noticed that Temara had two small lumps, one on either side of her groin. The lumps were about the size of a 20-cent coin and were quite firm but not overly sensitive to the touch. After consulting with Perth Zoo vets, they were diagnosed as enlarged lymph nodes. Lymph nodes become enlarged when an animal is mounting a significant immune response to something. Our senior vet Simone said this was nothing to worry about and that it would have been surprising if we hadn't seen some body response to the dramatic change in Temara's environment.

The twelfth of January marked my last day in the jungle with Temara. Martina and I didn't go out until 10.00 am, as we needed to sort out some paperwork first thing in the morning. Sukila the cook made us our favourite breakfast, as she knew our time at BTP was coming to an end. Temara had already travelled and eaten quite a lot of fruit by the time we arrived in the jungle. She decided to give Martina and me a relaxing afternoon, as she really didn't move much at all after we arrived. Given she was in a massive tree with fruit in it, though, she didn't really have a reason to move.

I was absolutely overjoyed when later in the afternoon Temara found the Holy Grail of trees in the Sumatran jungle...a durian tree, the mother lode of all Indonesian fruits! Durians, the most famous Indonesian fruit, are about the size of a large pineapple, with a hard, prickly rind, a highly flavoured, pulpy flesh and a very unpleasant odour. Durians are known to 'taste like heaven and

Temara content while eating in the canopy

smell like hell'. You are meant to either love them or hate them, but being the compromising Libran I am, I just think they're okay. Martina was definitely not a fan and thought that they smelt like old feet. Unfortunately, the durians Temara had found were all small and unripe, and she didn't attempt to open any. I really hoped she would remember where the tree was and return in a few weeks to claim her prize.

Apart from the durian highlight, Martina and I spent most of the afternoon chatting away and eating rambutans. We then acted like five-year-olds and Martina filmed me pretending to be a bride, since Martina was getting married soon. I had a dirty old pillowcase as a veil and a bunch of rotting leaves as a bouquet. Poor Perizal thought we were crazy, and I was sure he would be pleased to have some peace and quiet once the eccentric white girls went back home to Australia.

I think all this silliness was actually me being in denial about having to say goodbye to my beloved Temara. But 4.00 pm arrived and Martina told me gently but firmly that the time had come. Temara was about 25 metres up a massive tree and part of me thought she might not even come down to see me. But she couldn't resist bananas and rambutans, so she slowly descended the tree. Temara was in one of her rare lovely moods in which she was actually a gentle and pleasant orangutan. She didn't snatch, she didn't try to hit me and she let me give her a good rub. Maybe she knew we were leaving.

I thought I might cry when I had to say goodbye, but when the time came it just didn't feel right to cry. Here was an orangutan I had worked with and loved for seven years, absolutely free in the jungle to do what she wanted when she wanted. She was adapting brilliantly to her new life and all I could do was smile as I left her to climb back up her massive fruit tree. I waved goodbye, turned around and I didn't look back.

As I headed towards the station with Martina, I felt a huge sense of achievement. Temara had done her species proud and had proven that zoo-born orangutans do have a place in the jungle from which their ancestors were taken. I was very satisfied with what Temara had accomplished in such a short time, and I felt honoured that I was by her side during the first part of her remarkable world-first journey.

In the Indonesian language, the word 'orangutan' literally means 'person of the forest'. Temara was now indeed a person of the forest and living in her true home.

Farewell, Temara

16

Back to the real world

I had a lot of equipment to take back with me to Perth. Martina was flying home on a different airline, so I was desperately trying to condense or get rid of items I was somehow supposed to fit in my backpack. Some of the technicians tried to help me out in this area, since they wanted all my stuff anyway. One of the boys offered to buy my head torch with rupiah that equated to about $1.20. Considering mine cost $69 I said no! A few nights earlier, after dinner, Martina and I played them a DVD with Temara on it. Afterwards I said to Martina, 'Great, now they'll want to buy the laptop off me for $9.95'. I don't think the zoo would have been very impressed with that, considering it was their laptop!

Travelling from the BTP site back home to Australia takes two days, but these two days are exhausting and seem to last an eternity. Martina and I got up at 6.00 am on the day we left BTP to finish our packing. The definition of packing in this case was rolling, squeezing and stuffing all our things into every tiny orifice our bags still offered. I nearly got a hernia trying to do the zip up on my main bag. Plus I didn't fall asleep until after 3.00 am because I had already started to develop separation anxiety from Temara. I was also still sick from a horrible cold, and my rash/welts/bites were back in full force, so I spent all night scratching. When Sabine went to the loo in the middle of the night she thought she heard someone calling Temara, so it was probably me calling out her name in what little sleep I got. So I was not feeling or looking my best when we left BTP at 8.00 am.

The previous transports in and out of BTP had an average of six breakdowns per journey. We were praying we would make it to Jambi in time to check in to the Novotel, have actual showers with running water and be able to go to Pizza Hut for dinner. An hour and a half into the journey, that didn't look very likely. It had rained heavily the previous day and the mud road was in appalling condition. Before long we were bogged. The jeep was on a 45-degree angle and the back door was practically level with the mud in the huge ditch we were stuck in. Marty and I looked at each other and our faces dropped, since the thought of missing out on pizza seemed quite tragic. But never fear, those BTP vehicles are built tough. The front winch system was attached to a nearby tree and, amazingly, inch by inch the jeep slowly emerged from the massive mud pit in which it had been stuck.

So off we went again, with Marty and me grinning from ear to ear – until a massive plume of smoke from the engine completely covered the front windscreen. We really did think we were in trouble then, but two of the technicians travelling with us ran to a nearby creek, filled a large container with water and revived the radiator. Back on the road again and we finally reached what was heaven to us...the Novotel. Both of us jumped in the shower

The perilous journey back to Jambi City

(separately, of course) and did lots of girly things, including facial scrubs and a deep conditioning treatment for our hair. Then it was time for a dinner at Pizza Hut that didn't include rice or spinach, and I finished up with chocolate in the hotel room.

Then Sunday came. Getting from Jambi to Perth is never a fun journey. The first leg, to Jakarta, we took together. We drew solace from the fact that we weren't flying on the domestic airline that had crashed one week earlier in Indonesia. Our flight was delayed by two hours, and we were stuck in a small waiting area with about 580 other people and four rickety portable cool-air blowers that were basically useless.

Once we finally boarded the flight, I found that my seat wouldn't stay in the upright position. I tried to steady myself during take-off and keep the seat upright by gripping onto both armrests. This was a bad move, as the middle armrest wasn't secure either, and flew up in the air. The flight also had quite a bit of turbulence and our bladders were close to bursting, so it was not a very enjoyable experience. We were more than relieved when the plane landed.

We finally made it to Jakarta International Airport only for Martina to be told that her flight had been rescheduled to the next day. She managed to hold off having a nervous breakdown and somehow was transferred to another flight for that night, a few hours earlier than mine. While Martina was dealing with that, I was searching for painkillers to help subdue a nasty headache I had developed. Of course I couldn't find them, so I ended up on the airport floor, on my hands and knees, delving into my bag, which weighed about 56.7 kilograms, frantically searching for them. While searching my bag, I discovered that my mango shower gel had leaked all through my toiletries bag, so that it was all sticky and my bag smelt like a fruit smoothie. Why on earth didn't I just leave my mango shower gel at BTP? Between my dirty boots, exploded toiletries and my smelly dirty washing bag, I thought that if customs officials in Australia checked my bag, they would literally pass out and then hold me for questioning.

I soon waved Martina off as she boarded her flight and tried to stay awake for another three hours before I was able to board mine. I didn't want to fall asleep in case someone tried to saunter off with my luggage trolley full of mango-smelling, overweight bags. I finally made it home and on my first day back I was sick with a bad belly. The dodgy food choices on the flight home were beef rendang or fish curry. It was ridiculous that I had been in the Sumatran jungle for nearly three months and was fine, but the plane food on the journey home made me sick. My bags of disgraceful-smelling washing would have to wait.

I was so excited to return home and see all of my friends, family, Cooper my beloved dog and, of course, all the Perth Zoo orangutans! It was strange not having Temara at the zoo. Obviously the other keepers weren't quite used to it either, as they often made up eleven items of behavioural enrichment instead of just ten. We still keep Temara on our orangutan stock sheet where we list which exhibit each orangutan inhabits, but instead of an exhibit number, Temara's states 'Jungle – Sumatra'. We also have Temara's handprint framed and hanging in the orangutan kitchen.

We didn't get an update on Temara for at least two weeks after I returned home, so I was getting quite anxious as I waited for news. The first update that came through, though, was very positive, so I was excited and relieved. Peter explained that a rotating shift system had been established with Temara's trackers to ensure that she was constantly followed from dawn until dusk. Temara would only ever venture onto the ground if the gaps in the canopy were too large to be bridged. She was also still sleeping in a nest every night, usually about 20 metres up in the canopy. She would often sleep in the same nest for numerous nights but would add fresh nesting material to it daily. Some people would say she was lazy to use the same nest for multiple nights, but I like to think she was just saving energy and maybe, just like me, she doesn't like making her own bed.

From November 2006 to April 2007, Temara's wild diet consisted of approximately 80 per cent fruit. This was excellent for a newly released orangutan. It is considered a success if a released orangutan eats a minimum of 40 per cent fruit in their diet. Temara's high figure would not have been an entirely true reflection of her foraging ability, since there had been a massive fruiting season. This made it easy to find fruits, and large amounts of fruit were easy to collect. During this time, Temara showed very little interest in her trackers and did not beg for food or chase staff who had food, as some other released orangutans were doing. The next phase of Temara's release was for her to adapt to environmental conditions during the non-fruiting dry season.

While I was at BTP with Temara, she did not choose to interact with other orangutans. When other orangutans approached her, she would often become agitated and show mild aggression. We had hoped she would spend some time observing more experienced released orangutans to learn new forest skills. In an update report on Temara in May, we discovered that she was following a young female orangutan at a distance and watching her. Temara observed this orangutan eating new fruits and bark, which I hoped would assist her in exploiting more varied food sources in the upcoming dry season.

Update reports also outlined that Temara still had a small home range due to her very restricted moving pattern. Since her release, her feeding strategy appeared to be to remain in a small area, exploit all of its food resources until they were gone and then move on. She would need to travel more to find enough food sources once the fruiting season was over in May. Temara's trackers had to monitor her food intake very closely in the dry season, to ensure her calorie intake was sufficient to keep her healthy. During her first dry season, she was given two boiled eggs a day and some other supplementary food when she would take it.

During early June 2007, Temara began to sleep into the early afternoon before she commenced foraging. Wild orangutans begin to forage in the early morning and generally have a rest in the middle of the day. Temara appeared to be behaving more like a lazy human teenager with her extensive sleep-ins. Her trackers lured her to a different location with more forest fruit to try to break this habit. Unfortunately, by the time they reached their destination, the numerous mango trees in that area had recently stopped fruiting and had dropped their fruits. The rotting fruit on the ground provided a feast for a group of wild pigs and Temara watched them in fascination. I was pleasantly surprised to hear that she didn't throw anything at them.

After moving to this new location, Temara and the trackers were near the young orangutan play group that used this area for forest school. This particular forest school group consisted of Mona, Ali, Nyoman and Bona. Unlike Temara, these young orangutans, with some guidance from their babysitters, had been at the mango trees for some time and had eaten very well. The young orangutans in forest school were all excellent at finding fruit, and seemed to be intrigued to have Temara in their area. The curious foursome would often go to Temara's nest once she had settled down for a siesta in the middle of the day. This did not impress Temara at all. The disturbance would often prompt her to move out of her nest and observe what her young counterparts were doing from a distance. I was quite excited that Temara was spending time in proximity to younger orangutans with well-developed forest skills. It would be vital for her to still manage to find fruits in the dry season, as well as other nutritious food such as termites to keep her in good condition.

The final phase of Temara's release was for her to be able to live completely independently in the jungle. This could only be assessed properly after two full years in the BTP jungle. This time frame gives an accurate overview of whether an orangutan can survive during two non-fruiting seasons by exploiting various food sources. If this is proven to be the case, the orangutan is no longer followed. We were going to use this assessment with Temara and that meant, of course, that she would be followed for at least two years. Perth Zoo staff would travel to BTP twice a year to check on her progress and physical condition, and she would continue to be tracked by the Indonesian technicians on a daily basis. If Temara succeeded in the jungle, it would provide the opportunity for other suitable young Perth Zoo orangutans to be released in BTP.

17

Attack of the lemur

Soon after my return home from Sumatra, Leif was in discussion with a film producer who was working on an orangutan documentary called *The Last Trimate*. This documentary was to be about Dr Birute Galdikas and her work with orangutans in Borneo over the last thirty years. Along with Dian Fossey who studied gorillas and Jane Goodall who studied chimpanzees, Dr Galdikas was known as a 'Trimate' – one of the three most prominent researchers on primates. All of these women were chosen by the anthropologist Louis Leakey in the 1960s to research the great apes in Africa and Indonesia.

I had great respect for Dr Galdikas, who undertook years of research under very trying conditions at Tanjung Puting Reserve in Indonesian Borneo. She was a true pioneer. She was only twenty-five in 1971, when she arrived in Borneo with her husband, Rod, to begin her orangutan research. At this time, far less was known about the elusive orangutan than the African great apes.

Galdikas and her husband were based in a very basic small bark hut with a thatched roof, surrounded by a swamp forest. They named this site 'Camp Leakey' after Dr Leakey. Galdikas spent thousands of hours observing wild orangutans. She catalogued hundreds of types of orangutan foods, charted family histories for numerous wild orangutan units, mapped home ranges and gathered data on social interactions. I would devour fascinating stories told by Dr Galdikas in her books and journal articles. These included her coming face to face with a huge adult male orangutan as he travelled along the ground, observing orangutan infants throwing tantrums in the canopy and dodging branches thrown at her by orangutans high above.

Dr Galdikas' time in Borneo took on a new twist when the Indonesian Forestry Service asked if their camp in Tanjung Puting Reserve could be developed into an orangutan rehabilitation centre. From there it was envisaged that ex-captive orangutan youngsters could be reintroduced to life in the wild. And so began years of sharing their hut with confiscated infant and juvenile orangutans that had been so cruelly taken from their murdered mothers and kept as pets. These young orangutans were taken into the forest regularly with Dr Galdikas so they could learn the skills needed to live in the jungle on their own. Orangutan youngsters may be gorgeous, but they are not ideal houseguests, and Dr Galdikas and Rod had to contend with countless antics from the youngsters before they built an orangutan-proof house. These stories would have me in stitches. Dr Galdikas appeared on the cover of *National Geographic* in 1975. The photo of her with two juvenile orangutans in her care is still one of my favourite cover photos on this iconic publication.[8]

I was lucky enough to meet Dr Galdikas on location in Indonesia as well as in Australia when she participated in a great ape conservation lecture tour in 2005. I greatly enjoyed the time I was able to spend with her and hoped that she wouldn't tire of the questions I fired at her. When Dr Galdikas was in Perth, she visited Perth Zoo to see our world-famous orangutan colony. Because Dr Galdikas' experience with orangutans was so extensive, Leif and I took her to visit Puteri and Temara in their exhibit. A news crew filmed this experience in order to promote the lecture tour.

Despite Dr Galdikas' calm and gentle nature, Puteri did not seem very fond of her and appeared to be jealous of her being with Leif! Puteri has always had a soft spot for Leif and would hoot submissively at him and initiate cuddles. Puteri did not seem to approve of this 'other woman' being brought into the exhibit. Meanwhile, I had my hands full trying to ensure that the rambunctious Temara didn't embarrass all of us on the nightly news by causing a scene. I fed Temara a continual supply of dried figs that I had stuffed into every pocket of my zoo uniform. I think this indulgent food treat was the only thing that persuaded Temara not to run over to Leif and Birute and give them a hefty whack for spending time with her mother. It was definitely a case of 'Like mother, like daughter' with these two when it came to jealousy.

Dr Galdikas greatly enjoyed her time with the orangutans at Perth Zoo and praised the high level of care they received. Like an excited fan at a rock concert, I asked her to sign my copy of her book *Reflections of Eden* for me. She wrote 'To Kylie, in great gratitude for the love you share with the apes in your care!'

The producer of *The Last Trimate* documentary had contacted Leif because he wanted to feature Temara's release in the documentary about Dr Galdikas. This would allow the plight of the critically endangered Sumatran orangutan to be highlighted, with Temara as the species ambassador at BTP.

I was to leave for Sumatra to meet the film crew on 8 May 2007. Final preparations, including the booking of tickets, were being made on 5 May, and then disaster struck! While working at the zoo, I was helping another keeper out with feeding a group of ring-tailed lemurs. As I entered the enclosure with a container of grapes, two lemurs jumped towards me at the same time for their favourite food. The grapes were obviously irresistible and the lemurs had a very brief squabble. It only lasted for a split second and I didn't think much of it. My brain then registered that my right wrist felt rather warm, and I looked down to see a fountain of blood shooting up from it. I stayed calm and had enough sense to reduce the blood flow with my other hand and hold my bleeding wrist above my head. I made my way back immediately to the primate office with the other keeper, leaving a trail of blood behind me. After receiving some basic first aid from a workmate and trying not to faint, I was driven by Martina to the nearest hospital.

I was actually rather excited. I'd always wanted stitches, and that was all I thought I needed. And it would be a good story to tell – my first bite wound after working with primates for eight years, even if it was from a very cute and non-vicious-looking lemur. Most zookeepers have one scar or another after years in the industry. I started to realise that all was not well when a surgeon asked me to move my thumb and yet, as much as I tried, nothing happened. When a nurse said they'd have to book theatre I started to panic. I thought I'd better let my parents know, so I asked Marty to call my dad on his mobile. Marty opened with the line, 'Hi, Mr Bullo, it's Martina. Don't panic, but I'm just at the hospital with Kylie'. By this stage I suddenly had the urge to faint and had to be rescued by a passing orderly. I managed to score a bed – which is a rare commodity in a hospital these days. The plastic surgeon who was going to operate on me was inconveniently operating on someone else at the time, so my surgery kept being delayed. The worst part about the delay in my surgery was the fact that I hadn't eaten at all that day (that will teach me for not being a breakfast person) and I was starving. I had to sit next to people receiving their lunch and dinner, and to me, hospital food, just like plane food, smells utterly fabulous!

I was finally wheeled away to the operating theatre at 7.00 pm – just as I was ready to watch my favourite TV show. All of the surgical staff in the operating room were very interested in my injury. When I told them I worked with orangutans, they all assumed an orangutan had bitten me. While defending my darling Orange Kids and saying they would never do such a thing, I was a bit embarrassed when I then had to describe the cute, fluffy 3-kilogram primate that was responsible for severing the tendons in my wrist. Only the week before, I had taken a small film crew in with the ring-tailed lemurs at the zoo for a TV segment. The presenter was a bit nervous of the lemurs. As one of them leapt past her head, she let out a squeal and asked, 'Do they ever bite, Kylie?' I answered decisively with, 'Oh no, of course not, they're very gentle'. I must have jinxed myself.

Dr Paul Quinn, my surgeon, was lovely and made me feel at ease right away. He asked me numerous questions about what had happened and asked me to move my thumb, but again, there was no reaction when I tried to move it. He then removed the bandage, but parts of it had stuck in the two slash wounds from the lovely lemur's teeth. Oh my God, profanities rang out as the bandage was peeled off, and I nearly crushed the poor nurse who had offered me her hand to hold. Dr Quinn said there looked to be quite serious damage to the tendons and nerves. Consequently, when I asked him if I could fly to Sumatra in three days to film a documentary, he looked at me with sympathy and said, 'I think you'll still be in hospital in three days, sweetie'. It was then that I burst into tears in the operating room.

There had been a lot of damage indeed. Two tendons were severed in two places, a third tendon was also severed, a major nerve was severed along three branches and there was also muscle damage. All this from a lemur! I couldn't believe it. Neither could my workmates. Although they gave me lots of support and sympathy, they also thought it was quite hilarious that a lemur had put me in hospital for more than four hours of microsurgery. They came to visit me in hospital the next day, bearing gifts – one of which, purchased from the Perth Zoo gift shop, was a soft toy ring-tailed lemur. They had cut his right hand off, stitched up the severed arm and put red texta on it to make it look like blood. Bless my darling friends!

The toy lemur took pride of place on my hospital bedside table, along with an overdose of flowers and cards from concerned friends and family. I was at a teaching hospital, so when the doctor on duty came to do rounds and check on me, so did seven medical students. They were all very interested in 'the girl who was mauled by a monkey'. None of them knew what a ring-tailed lemur was, so rather than explain it to them, I would just point gingerly to the soft toy with my bandaged-up arm. Suddenly their expressions would change from a blank stare to a nod of acknowledgement… and then without fail they would start singing 'I like to move it, move it' from the movie *Madagascar*. I now hate that song with a passion.

The injury proved extremely painful and quite debilitating. I was basically left one-handed, and my right hand and wrist were

Recuperating after surgery with my matching injured lemur soft toy

highly sensitive to touch. My protective sock-like bandage had to be changed three days after leaving the hospital. My thumb had to slot through a hole and the sock bandage went up my arm. This seemed simple enough, or so I thought. My dad was my designated nurse. We didn't even succeed in taking the bandage off because I was squealing and squirming around too much, so Dad ended up having to cut the sock bandage off. I tried not to vomit while he cleaned the wound area and yelled at my mum, who was trying to take photos of the saga for one of her many photo albums on my zoo life. Even Cooper was stressed, and he wanted to lick my bandaged arm to make it feel better.

We then had to somehow put a new sock bandage on. This took thirty minutes. No matter how my dad tried to put the bandage over my hand, it was agony and felt hideous because of the nerve damage. I was in tears and trying not to belt my poor dad over the head and run out of the room screaming. Dad finally lost his patience and spoke to me like I was a five-year-old being forced to eat my vegetables. I sat there and pouted, but in one fell swoop Dad then got the bandage on. We both agreed that to preserve our mental health and father–daughter relationship we weren't doing that ever again and we would get a nurse to do the next bandage-change at my first check-up. And with that we opened a bottle of red wine to calm all our nerves. I don't think I was meant to drink cabernet merlot with my pain-relief medication, but I didn't care at that point.

My wrist injury was very extensive and painful, and it was a long road to recovery. Hand therapy and visiting my specialist became normal weekly activities. I also had to move back home with my parents for three weeks, since I couldn't even do simple things by myself such as have a shower. One night Mum was helping me prepare for a shower in their bathroom. I had to wear a big plastic cover over my arm bandage to prevent it getting wet in the shower. Mum turned around to put this plastic cover on my arm at the same time that I turned around to place something on the sink. The impact was quick but excruciating. Mum's body bumped into my arm and I swore my head off in agony as electric shocks and pain shot up my arm due to the severe nerve and tendon damage. My poor mum burst into tears and then I burst into tears since I had made my mum cry. I started to apologise for yelling and then she hugged me, all while I was butt naked. My dignity was somewhere on the bathroom floor, along with the crumpled bathmat.

The injury started to drive me crazy pretty quickly. I couldn't do a lot one-armed and while I was in pain. I was also bored but couldn't sleep at night since it felt like thousands of spiders were climbing up my arm. Luckily, I could return to work on a gradual basis quite quickly because I was acting supervisor of primates at the time, and this was mostly office work. I visited the ring-tailed lemurs to say hi, but only from the safety of outside their exhibit. I became quite adept at typing and writing with my left hand, but I never mastered the art of doing my hair one-handed.

My morning tea and lunch breaks at work amused everyone, as I had to do my hand-strengthening exercises. I also had to desensitise the two large scars on my right wrist to the touch, since this was where the nerve damage was located. When I was at my hand-therapy sessions, the therapists would massage my wrist to desensitise it. I would try not to cry, swear or abuse them, because the pain was just unbearable at times. The therapists knew that patients found it very difficult to actually massage scars with their own hands and that it was often easier to use another object to do this. In my case they gave me a mini vibrating massager. I tended to only use this at home, since I knew all my workmates would give me grief about it. One night, though, a big group of us was out for dinner. I was showing my new handbag to my friend Holly and she was admiring the internal pockets. And then she found it. The next thing I knew, my mini massager was vibrating down the table in the restaurant to shrieks of laughter from all my friends. The more I protested that it was for my wrist, the more they teased me about it. After that night, I used the vibrating massager every day at work, as I figured it couldn't get any more embarrassing than that night out at dinner. I was also desperate to regain the full use of my hand and thumb, and desensitise my scars.

The trip to Sumatra to film the documentary was rescheduled for mid-July. This was eleven weeks post-injury, and I would be nearly out of the danger period in terms of my tendons possibly rupturing. I didn't want to jinx anything so close to leaving again, and I considered sitting in a padded room so I couldn't injure myself. But all went well and we left for Jakarta on 18 July 2007.

18

Documentary, jungle style

The film crew consisted of the producer Stephen, cameraman Peter and sound technician Morgan. We flew from Perth to Jakarta and then flew to Jambi the following day. I always get a bit worried being on the small internal flights within Indonesia. When they do the safety demonstration I actually check to see if the life jacket is under my seat. This has probably been prompted by the fact that on the food tray in front of you it says, 'Please do not remove life jacket from plane unless in an emergency', which obviously means there are quite a few passengers out there who think the life jacket as well as the orange juice is complimentary on the flight.

I think I stressed Morgan out by telling him all my travel-sickness stories and that I had yet again forgotten to bring travel-sickness medication with me. This was not good for Morgan, since he was sitting next to me. I saw him shift in his seat to be as far away from me as possible. We made it to Jambi and then had to collect all of the film crew's equipment – and there was a lot of it. We then made our way to our hotel and met Peter Pratje for dinner. We also met with a police official to negotiate hiring the police helicopter. The film crew wanted to obtain footage of the national park and surrounding areas, including oil palm plantations, from the helicopter.

We made an early start the next day to travel to the release site. It was a four-hour road trip to the town of Tebo and I kept my eyes shut for most of it. This was firstly to avoid feeling carsick and secondly so I didn't have to look at the usual near-miss head-on collisions with an oncoming truck laden with oil palm fruit every ten minutes or so. Tebo was the changeover point and transport hub for the Wildlife Protection Units. Not many Westerners ever go through Tebo, so lots of kids either ran up to us and stared or ran away in terror and hid behind their mothers. They would freak out when I spoke Indonesian to them, so the best way to make friends with them would be to join in a game of soccer or offer them lollies. I've always found Indonesian kids highly adorable.

After about an hour we were ready to leave for the treacherous road leading to BTP. We had to take two of the Toyota 4WDs out to the site due to the supplies we had to take with us and about 894 kilograms of filming equipment. The film crew and I were in the back of an enclosed jeep, and the other vehicle was a pick-up with most of the supplies on the back. The journey started off well but only lasted about seventeen minutes before our jeep broke down. Despite the dirt road leading to BTP only being 35 kilometres, it can take anywhere from two hours to four days to reach the release site, depending on the condition of the road and vehicles. I was really hoping the film crew wouldn't have to endure a four-day trek to the site!

Our jeep continued to break down every couple of kilometres, and with about 5 kilometres to go it gave up and went on strike. It was 8.00 pm and dark, so we all had to transfer to the 4WD pick-up. We would have been arrested in Australia, since there were eleven people in and on the pick-up vehicle in total – three in the front cab and eight on the tray. Cameraman Peter sat in the passenger seat with his precious rented camera that was worth $200,000. Due to my arm still being in a removable splint for protection, I was unable to go on the back of the vehicle because I couldn't grip onto the bar. So that meant that I ended up in the front cab, sitting on a 20-kilogram bag of rice, in between the cameraman and the driver, with my legs on either side of the gearstick. Luckily, we pretty much stayed in first gear for the rest of the trip, otherwise I might have had to slap the driver!

And so we began a two-hour drive over the last 5 kilometres to get to the release site. It was the worst trip into BTP I had experienced, but I think it was exacerbated by the fact that it was dark and things always seem worse in the dark. My position in the cab was ungraceful and highly uncomfortable. Not only was I trying not to get flung through the windscreen during the extremely rough ride, since there was no seatbelt, I was desperately trying to protect my arm from being knocked and injured again. I ended up in the driver's lap on more than one occasion, but thankfully I didn't get flung onto the $200,000 camera.

I felt even worse for the rest of the film crew on the back of the pick-up, as it began to rain. Soon we reached the main river we had to cross and everyone on the back of the vehicle hung on for dear life. Unfortunately, our bags didn't have the ability to grip tighter, and four of them fell off into the river. Of course mine was one of them. A couple of the technicians travelling with us managed to fish them out but they were sopping wet. 'Not to worry, that will be covered by my travel insurance', I thought. As I thought about it for another minute I realised, 'Hang on…I didn't bloody get travel insurance, I totally forgot'. I suddenly felt panic. I couldn't believe I had forgotten to take out travel insurance. Here I was in the middle of nowhere, recovering from a serious injury, prone to having an allergic reaction to bee stings, my bag now soaked, and I had *no* travel insurance. I gulped and chanted to myself, 'Do not fall over, do not get lost, do not get stung by bees and do not stack it and rupture your nearly healed tendons'.

We finally made it to the release site at about 11.00 pm and headed to the little kitchen, where everyone was waiting for us. The cooks made us some noodles and they tasted delicious! Mind you, I would have eaten cardboard by that stage, I was so hungry. After scoffing down our noodles we all staggered off to bed to try to get some sleep before the first day of filming.

When we met up for breakfast the next morning, Stephen explained to me that they wanted to capture a moving reunion between Temara and me on film. Stephen was envisaging sunlight streaming through the canopy and Temara climbing down the tree to come and see me. I think he was also hoping for a hug of some sort between Temara and me. I tried to break the news gently that Temara might not even come down and if she did then any physical contact we had would probably involve Temara trying to stab me with her thumbnail, bless her cottons!

Temara was located about forty-five minutes away from the station on foot. As we got closer to her location, I couldn't stop grinning. I was both excited and nervous about seeing her after her six months of living in the jungle. As soon as I called out Temara's name, she came straight down to visit me. She reached her arm down to make contact and I reached up and held her hand. I felt special because it was at least seventeen seconds before she stuck her thumbnail into my hand. Temara was a bit wary of the film crew, but she was prepared to stay down low in the canopy and let me touch her once she saw that I had some decent treats. I had brought some natural licorice with me from Perth, and Temara loves licorice! I also had some little Indonesian bananas, and Temara was quite demanding with wanting food treats. As I gave Temara some treats, she let me check her physical condition. She was in excellent condition, and her coat had become much darker and glossier.

The producer didn't want me to wear my blue protective arm splint for the filming. My right wrist was still very tender and the back of my hand and thumb were totally numb since the nerves

Checking Temara's teeth and gums

had been severed. I therefore tried to interact with Temara with my left hand. There was absolutely no way I wanted Temara to touch my hypersensitive right hand with her thumbnail and cause me to swear on camera. Initially, it was difficult to do the filming, but Stephen asked me questions, which got me chatting away and feeling more relaxed. After about twenty minutes, Temara began to get impatient and wanted the small amount of remaining food. I warned the film crew that their time was nearly up. Just before they stopped filming, in true Temara style, she had a tantrum. She tried to hit me and shook the branches above my head in protest against the banana I hadn't given to her. I cracked up laughing and told her how cranky she was. And of course that scene made it to the documentary. Oh well, that's why I love Temara so much – she has such personality and will always make it well known if she isn't happy about something.

After we stopped filming I could relax and just sit on the ground and observe Temara in the jungle. I felt a tremendous sense of satisfaction and happiness while watching her travel and forage in the canopy. She was actually living in the jungle. The first-ever zoo-born orangutan to be released into the wild, and look at her! I was so proud of her and honoured that I was the one to help her make it here. An added bonus to my already exciting day was learning that Temara was very close to another adult female named Mena with a newborn female infant. The trackers said Temara had been following and watching Mena for a couple of days and seemed very interested in her and the baby. I was stoked to hear this, since Temara was now a sexually mature female and it was very encouraging that she was showing an interest in Mena and the baby.

But yet again, in true Temara style, she couldn't be polite for an extended period of time. She tentatively moved into the tree

Mena occupied and sauntered slowly across a branch so that she was within arm's reach. I thought Mena was being very tolerant of Temara. Then, in a flash, Temara reached out and poked the baby. Orangutan mothers are highly protective of their infants, and Temara's inappropriate actions resulted in Mena hitting her and chasing her away. This was the first time I had ever seen Temara put in her place, and I stifled a laugh.

I was only in BTP with the film crew for a few days, so I spent as much time as I could observing Temara in the jungle. I continued to be impressed by her skills in the forest. She was certainly well on her way to proving that a mentally and physically healthy zoo-born orangutan could adapt to jungle life, and I was excited about what the future held.

19

Where's the vomit bag?

I travelled to Sumatra to assess Temara again in August 2008 with one of the supervisors of the exotic section at Perth Zoo named Trueman. Leif and Clare had checked on Temara in early 2008. Perth Zoo staff were checking on Temara twice a year and an orangutan keeper would always make the trek over to assess her. Travelling with Trueman brought out one of my worst travelling traits – vomiting! I've had the travel sickness trait from a very young age. Day trips with my family often resulted in my poor mum being relegated to the back seat so I could sit in the front to help ease my travel sickness. A plethora of travel sickness supplies would also come on the journey, including buckets, Minties and tea-tree oil to help with the smell of vomit. As everyone knows, the smell of vomit initiates sympathetic vomiting, so that had to be avoided at all costs. After a while, Mum came up with the philosophy 'What doesn't go down can't come back up', so I would often spend the journey hungry!

Knowing that I'm highly prone to travel sickness, I never drink alcohol when I fly. Never, that is, until I travelled with Trueman. We had a couple of hours to wait until we boarded our flight, so Trueman suggested we have a drink at the bar. I was going to order a Diet Coke but with a nudge from Trueman I was soon ordering a nice glass of merlot. Once we were on the plane I also ordered a merlot with dinner. 'This is the life', I thought. 'I'm finally having a free wine on a plane flight like normal people'. It also helped to wash away the taste of the plane meal.

Thirty minutes after dinner I was reading a book and settling into the flight when a wave of nausea passed over me. I told myself to stop being silly – this was an international flight and I didn't vomit on international flights on huge planes. I only vomited on small domestic flights. Then the awful flashbacks came: one was vomiting in a small country town airport in Western Australia after just making it off the plane in time; the other one was in Kalimantan when I was travelling with Leif on a TOP tour. The flight was one hour long and I felt nauseous for fifty-seven minutes of it. I was sitting near the window and Leif was sitting next to me, talking about the strategic plan for TOP. I was trying to listen to Leif and silently chanting my 'Don't vomit, don't vomit' mantra. I started to get sweaty palms and that horrible saliva build-up in my mouth that indicates vomiting is inevitable. My mum's voice was in my head: 'Just think positive, just think positive'. I'm sure that if not feeling nauseous were that easy there would be no market for travel-sickness medication.

I eyed off the vomit bag in the seat pocket in front of me and thought, 'Seriously, how does one of those things actually work?'

Surely it would just disintegrate, and it didn't look all that big. I started to panic. I tried to slow my breathing and I closed my eyes as the plane descended quickly. As the wheels hit the tarmac I thought, 'Yes, I made it', followed by, 'Oh my God, I still need to vomit'. In one swift motion I grabbed that vomit bag and filled it! I was sure everyone on the plane could hear me heaving, and I was so embarrassed but relieved at the same time.

As the plane slowed down, Leif proceeded to say to me, 'Are you going to get rid of the vomit?' We were not disembarking. More people had to get on the plane before we made the next leg of the journey. My head was still spinning and I rested my forehead against the cool of the plane window. I told Leif that I couldn't get up since I still felt dizzy. His next words surprised me.

'Give me the vomit.'

'No', I replied, horrified.

Leif responded with, 'Give me the bag of vomit'.

'No, I'm too embarrassed', I said.

Leif retorted with, 'Well, it's not coming with us on the next flight'.

With that I sheepishly handed him my bag of vomit, which he proceeded to hold out in the middle of the plane aisle. Thankfully, a flight attendant came past just at that moment to take it far, far away. I slunk down in my seat and closed my eyes, dreading the next leg of the flight.

And now here I was, three years later, on another orangutan trip with a different zoo colleague and I had the urge to vomit. Given how badly the other experience had turned out, and having thrown two glasses of red wine into the equation, I knew I was in trouble. But even worse, there were *no* vomit bags in any of the seat pockets in my row. I tapped Trueman on the shoulder and told him of my predicament. He had a bit of a chuckle, but when he saw my eyes bulge and my hands cover my mouth, an expression of terror crossed his face. With no vomit bag in sight he was in my line of fire. Without wasting another second, Trueman delved into his backpack and pulled out a paper bag he'd obtained at the newsagency when he bought a magazine. He thrust it at me just as the inevitable happened. Let me just say, a newsagency paper bag is no match for a thick, foil-lined industrial-strength airline vomit bag. Before the flimsy paper bag even had a chance to disintegrate above my lap, Trueman grabbed it and frantically pressed the call button for a flight attendant, while the guy next to me pressed himself against the window, as far away from me as possible. I sunk back into my seat and wondered why on earth I hadn't packed travel-sickness tablets for this trip and how I thought drinking wine was appropriate given my travel record!

I came to regret not packing the travel-sickness tablets the next day as well. Being the short arse I am, I always draw the short straw when it comes to my position in the car. On the long winding journey to the car changeover point to get into BTP, my travel sickness hit with full force. Poor Trueman was yet again stuck next to nauseous Kylie. I managed to get out of the car just in time for yet another vomiting episode, this time on the border of an oil palm plantation. I actually felt quite satisfied vomiting on an oil palm tree, and hoped that it would die.

I was extremely relieved once we changed over into the hardcore Toyota 4WD and hit the rough dirt roads to get to BTP. Despite being a very rough journey, the car travels slowly and there are too many breakdowns and bogging episodes to ever get carsick. In true BTP travel style, we broke down about five times, but Trueman became Mr Miyagi the mechanic's sidekick as he helped tinker with the engine and use bush-mechanic medicine to fix the 4WD.

Another risk factor when travelling to the release site is the numerous makeshift bridges that need to be crossed. Sometimes all these so-called bridges consisted of were a few logs for each tyre to perilously creep over to get to the other side. I used to bite my lip and hold my breath every time we crossed one of these bridges, and only exhale once we made it across. Tragically, later that year, there was a fatality while a vehicle was crossing one of the worst bridges after heavy rains. After this event, when travelling to BTP, Perth Zoo staff had to walk over the bridges and then wait for the 4WD to cross. This eliminated any risk to us of being in an accident while in the vehicle, but we were still always nervous for the driver as he meticulously made his way over the bridges, guided by his colleagues on the other side.

One of many perilous bridges leading into BTP

It had been a year since I had seen Temara, so I was extremely excited to see her. I also felt proud that Trueman was able to see Temara, even if he wasn't an 'ape man'. Trueman had worked in the zoo industry for more than twenty years, primarily with ungulates and carnivores. He was a great travelling companion, as he was very practical and remained calm in a crisis. Plus he would constantly make me laugh, and when you're in the hot, sweaty jungle, a good laugh is always welcome. We made the time pass more quickly when Temara was sleeping by filming stupid skits on camera, including David Attenborough impersonations, practising our Indonesian and feeding the chilli from our lunch to the tribes of ants that inhabited most of our sitting sites. The ants also took a strange liking to the bright-blue elastic bands that held our lunchboxes closed. As soon as we placed an elastic band on a log, a gang of ants would make a beeline for it and start carrying it away, ecstatic with their new find. Trueman and I found this fascinating, so we would bring extra elastic bands with us so we could be entertained by the foraging ants.

It was fantastic to see Temara again and spend some time doing jungle observations on her. She was in good physical condition and she came down readily to see me. She also appeared quite relaxed, as she lazed about in the canopy for an afternoon siesta. On one afternoon I observed some fascinating behaviour. A Sumatran flying squirrel was foraging about in the canopy and then entered Temara's tree. I expected her to fly into a rage, since she had always been terrified if a native possum managed to take up residence in her Perth Zoo exhibit. But Temara remained very calm and watched the squirrel with curiosity. She certainly was adapting to her new forest life and all the residents that shared her living space. It was wonderful to see this first-hand. She still tended to sleep in quite late, so I would find a comfortable position myself until she graced us with some activity.

Resting on the job while Temara sleeps in

We also visited the other release site at BTP, named Dano Alo. The site was absolutely stunning, with a pristine river, lovely wooden huts and breathtaking hills. The hills were breathtaking in more ways than one – both to look at and when trekking up them; I would often be out of breath, as I had to do my usual running to keep up with the Indonesian trackers. A new experience at this release site also included seeing fresh tiger tracks one morning, which was a highlight, especially for Trueman, who had worked with Sumatran tigers for years. The tiger tracks were quite close to camp, so I made sure the windows of my wooden hut were locked that night, even if it meant I was sweating profusely while trying to get to sleep.

Another highlight of 2008 was when world-renowned primatologist Dr Jane Goodall visited Australia to give lectures about her time spent studying wild chimpanzees in Gombe Stream National Park in Tanzania, and about her book *Reason for Hope*. Goodall is considered the world's foremost expert on chimpanzees. She is the founder of the Jane Goodall Institute (JGI) and the Roots & Shoots Program. JGI supports the chimpanzee research

Fresh tiger tracks on our jungle trek

at Gombe, while Roots & Shoots is a global youth program that strives to improve local environmental issues. She has also worked extensively on conservation and animal welfare issues.

I hold Jane Goodall in high regard. Her bravery and commitment as a young woman to studying the chimpanzees in Gombe in the 1960s are truly inspiring to me. Her research is well known for challenging two long-held beliefs of the day: that only humans could construct and use tools, and that chimpanzees were vegetarians. Jane observed a chimpanzee using stalks of grass to 'fish' for termites at a termite mound. The chimpanzee would place the grass in the termite holes, then remove it once it was covered with termites and proceed to eat them. The chimps were also seen modifying sticks by stripping them of leaves, to make a more effective tool. Humans had always thought we were the only species capable of making and using tools. In a now-famous quote in response to this discovery, Louis Leakey wrote, 'We must now redefine man, redefine tool, or accept chimpanzees as human'.[9]

I was thrilled to hear that Jane was including Perth on her upcoming lecture tour, and I could barely contain my excitement when I discovered she would be visiting the orangutans at Perth Zoo. Due to Jane's vast experience and knowledge of the great apes, Leif and I decided it would be safe to take Jane in with Puteri the orangutan for a painting session. Jane has a very gentle nature, and Puteri warmed to her immediately and was very keen to paint. Jane also greatly enjoyed the intimate experience with Puteri. All of the primate staff were honoured to meet Jane. We all agreed that she had a beautiful and calming yet inspiring aura. We felt invigorated and inspired to continue our conservation work after spending time with her.

Jane also signed my copy of *Reason for Hope* with 'For Kylie – Together we can make this a better world for all. Follow your heart'. I truly believe this.

Painting with Jane Goodall and Puteri

20

Skin-tight white T-shirts

Time certainly flies, and in August 2009 I was off to BTP again to check on Temara and help with the orangutan enrichment program. On this trip, one of my fellow orangutan keepers, Sam, came along for the first time to see the site and assist with the orangutan enrichment and training program. To say Sam was excited was an understatement, and her enthusiasm and excitement reminded me how lucky I was to be able to undertake these trips, which had somehow become a normal part of my life. As well as our usual plethora of luggage, including mosquito dome tents, blow-up mattresses, clothes, insect repellent, sleeping bags, lots of deodorant and other items, we also had the task of taking thirty-one large padlocks with us. These were going to be used to replace all of the old padlocks on the cages at the release site. Well, thirty-one padlocks in a box became extremely heavy very quickly. They also raised suspicion at every Indonesian airport where we disembarked. We had to open the box and show the inspectors that we weren't carrying drugs or explosives every time. They then had to reseal the box for us. So by the time we reached our destination, the innocent violated box was being held together by sticky tape. Sam and I were both relieved when the padlocks were put to good use at the release site.

On the way to BTP, we sadly passed the usual constant stream of trucks laden with either freshly cut tree trunks or oil palm fruits. The environmental devastation I always see in Indonesia can be soul-crushing. For every tree I fight to save, it seems 100 are massacred in its place. With the world's ever-growing population and demand for unsustainable resources, I sometimes wonder if the dedicated few in this world are fighting a losing battle. But we will keep fighting, since it is the only hope for the future of the orangutan. With no voice of their own, someone has to speak for them.

Sam discovered that the 4WD trip going into BTP is like driving in a bumper-car ring. She had a fair few bruises as proof from bouncing around in the back tray and being slammed into the metal bar we grip onto. Despite being a risky and rough ride it can also be quite exhilarating.

We worked with the technicians to create more behavioural enrichment for the caged orangutans that were being prepared for release. Most orangutan releases are done from November to January because that is when the fruiting season commences. It is imperative that orangutans in the cages are mentally stimulated and encouraged to undertake natural behaviours such as tool use while they are confined. We prepared an array of varied enrichment for the orangutans with the staff. These included pieces of fire hose stuffed with banana leaves and forest fruits, honey smeared in bamboo dipping poles, and fishing games. These new items kept the orangutans busy for extended periods, which was fantastic. The technicians were also very enthusiastic about providing these new items to the orangutans, so that was very positive.

Coincidently, Perth Zoo was going to launch its 'Don't Palm Us Off' campaign, run in conjunction with Melbourne Zoo, soon after Sam and I were due back at the zoo after our trip. This campaign aimed to bring in government legislation that would make it compulsory for companies to list palm oil in the ingredients of food products. This would enable consumers to make an informed choice about palm oil when they purchased products. As well as checking on Temara, we were asked by Perth Zoo's marketing department if it was possible to get some photos of Temara with the 'Don't Palm Us Off' slogan, to raise awareness for this important campaign. Sam and I were given white T-shirts and laminated signs with the 'Don't Palm Us Off' logo on them. The transfer logos were put on the T-shirts just before we left Perth, and I shoved the shirts in my bag in a mad rush without even looking at them properly.

We decided to do the photos during our first Temara visit. That way, if we weren't successful, we could try again another day. Before we started, I took the T-shirts out of my bag and my heart sank... they were tiny and looked like they had been shrunk in the wash or were made for anorexic teenage-girl models. How did they expect us to wear these? I wondered if they could somehow have magically shrunk due to the humidity. The T-shirts were size 8 and size 10, so I immediately kept the size 10 as Sam is tiny and the size 8 wouldn't have gone over my head. Sam was not impressed. We both squeezed into our Playboy-bunny-sized T-shirts and headed off on a one-hour trek with our tracker to find Temara.

When we finally reached Temara, Sam and I were sweaty, stinky, red-faced and puffing. Consequently, the already-tight T-shirts were clinging to us with sweat. It was highly unattractive. White is also by far the worst colour to wear in the jungle! I wanted to rest for ten minutes so I could cool down a bit and catch my breath before the photo shoot, but that wasn't to be, since Temara came racing down the tree to see me and was hanging low from a branch with her arm stretched out to me. It was either a sign of affection or she thought I would have some food treats for her. I was so thrilled to see Temara and I had to go over to her, since she had come down to see me. So the photo shoot consisted of Sam and me feeding Temara and holding up the 'Don't Palm Us Off' poster, with skin-tight white, sweaty T-shirts stuck to us. It was so disgusting and the sweat was just dripping down our backs and

Horrid skin-tight white T-shirt photo shoot with Temara

other places I won't mention. I wanted to wipe the sweat off my face but Temara would not let go of my arm, so I just had to stand next to her for ten minutes and have my photo taken looking like a feral, ugly, sweaty freak. Temara looked fantastic – her coat was so dark and lustrous and her face had matured. At least Temara would look good in the photos, I thought.

Sam hadn't met Temara before, as she had started working in the primate section just after Temara made her historic journey to the jungles of Sumatra, but she was excited and fascinated to observe how Temara had adapted to the wild. It was evident that she had transferred many skills she had developed at Perth Zoo to her new jungle life. These included nest building and using tools to obtain food and water. We both watched excitedly as Temara quickly and repeatedly poked a stick down a tree hollow to obtain fresh water. We provide this type of enrichment to the orangutans at Perth Zoo, so it was satisfying to see first-hand how our enrichment program promotes real behaviours that are necessary for survival in the wild.

After watching Temara for a few hours and taking notes on her activities and behaviour, we started the long trek back to camp in the late afternoon. Clouds that had seemed safely distant had quickly moved to be lurking above us, and within a few minutes the rain started pelting down. Rain in the jungle after a long, hot day isn't so bad, since it can be lovely and refreshing, but I'm usually wearing a normal-sized, dark-coloured shirt. Within an instant our inappropriate skin-tight white T-shirts had become see-through and were somehow stuck to us even more tightly. I don't know who was more embarrassed, us or the very modest Indonesian tracker who was leading us home. We ended up wearing our backpacks on our chests so the poor Indonesian boy could still look at us. We couldn't take those disgusting, foul-smelling tight T-shirts off quickly enough when we arrived back at camp. I stuffed my filthy wet offending T-shirt into a plastic bag and tried to forget that it ever existed.

As well as spending time observing and assessing Temara's adaptation, we were thrilled at being able to assist with orangutan forest school. Numerous young orangutans were taking part in regular forest school classes to learn how to survive in the forest. A particular young male orangutan named Mopi stole our hearts with his cheeky nature and enjoyment at being carried to and from his forest school lessons. He loved forest school so much that it actually took me, Sam and the tracker five minutes to 'catch' him one day, since he kept somersaulting down hills to ensure his forest school outing lasted longer. Once he had exhausted himself he was willing to have a piggyback ride back to the cage while munching on some sweet potato.

Another highlight of the trip for me was the fact that I had been upgraded to new accommodation! No longer was I sleeping in the dingy little room in the vet clinic that only had an outdoor toilet. A new wooden hut had been constructed to accommodate researchers and students at BTP, and by jungle standards I gave it a five-star rating – mainly due to the indoor toilet. That came to a very quick end, however, when we realised it was blocked. I cursed my small bladder every time I had to go outside to pee at night in the pitch black, praying that a Sumatran tiger didn't fancy human flesh on its menu that night.

Sam and I also visited the local school and I recognised quite a few of the children from my previous visits. We had brought more gifts for the children – from Temara, of course – and this collection included picture books, crayons, soft toys, animal puzzles and animal puppets. My Indonesian had improved quite a bit, so I spoke to the kids about the presents and how important

An excited babysitter helping to look after Mopi at jungle school

Luxury jungle accommodation

it was to look after the forest and Temara. We then played with the kids in the classroom with all of the new items and had a competition to see who could complete the puzzles the fastest. I think Indonesian kids are just beautiful, and it was fun to play with them and see them warm to us quite quickly. We stayed for their lunch break and played volleyball with them, which they thought was fabulous. I didn't think it was so fabulous, since I'm useless at volleyball and the scars on my right wrist from the lemur bite took a beating. We then had some group photos and all too quickly it was time to say goodbye to the gorgeous, smiling kids.

Visiting the local school

21

Sibling rivalry

After arriving home from Sumatra in September 2009, we were all eagerly awaiting the arrival of Temara's baby sibling, since her mother, Puteri, was heavily pregnant. This really was a miracle pregnancy, since Puteri had nearly died in 2008 due to a condition known as dysfunctional uterine bleeding. Puteri had passed numerous large blood clots and become very ill. The advice of a human gynaecologist named Dr Tony McCartney was sought to assist the vets with this very serious case. During Puteri's illness I came in to work one morning to find her extremely ill and almost unresponsive in her night den. She had passed numerous blood clots and I feared the worst. The vets were called immediately, and Puteri was taken to the vet department to be given fluids and other supportive treatments. Perth Zoo's vets and orangutan keepers contacted other zoos and the gynaecologist for advice. Since Puteri had lost so much blood, a hysterectomy was a possibility, but we wanted this to be only a last resort, since we wanted her to be able to breed again. It was decided to give Puteri a blood transfusion to save her life. An orangutan blood transfusion had not been done at Perth Zoo before, so we were all quite nervous.

We undertook this procedure in the evening. Puteri's full-blood sister Punya was anaesthetised, as it was likely that they were compatible for a blood transfusion and Punya was also a large orangutan. As well as receiving a blood transfusion, Puteri was given an iron injection and two injections of Depo-Provera, a human female contraceptive drug. Martina and I were up at the vet department until close to midnight as the vet team, led by Simone, worked tirelessly on Puteri. Martina and I also had to take blood samples into a hospital for testing. By midnight I was a nervous, teary wreck, but Marty remained stoic and held it together while I sobbed on her shoulder in fear that we would lose our beloved and gentle Puteri. She was returned to her night den late at night on a comfy bed of shredded paper and blankets. Keepers and vet staff reluctantly went home for a few hours of broken sleep once Puteri was settled in her den.

We arrived early the next morning to find Puteri gently stirring. She was very weak and exhausted after her procedure, but she was alive and fighting. It was only after Puteri got up and came over to her that Martina broke down in tears with the realisation that Puti might survive this traumatic event after all. Puteri continued to gain strength over the following weeks, and her famous appetite returned. Dr McCartney had told us in simple terms that there were two cures for Puteri's condition in human females: get pregnant or have a hysterectomy. Obviously we were hoping for the baby option! Once Puteri's condition had stabilised and she was in good health, we decided to put her with Hsing Hsing for breeding. We didn't expect much, since Puteri's menstruation had been very irregular since her life-threatening illness, but we thought we would give her a chance. The primate team was so grateful to the vet staff and Dr McCartney for saving Puteri's life. We now hoped that another miracle would occur and allow Puteri to fall pregnant.

Puteri was housed with Hsing Hsing for more than a year with no sign of pregnancy. I had been supervising the primate section for a few months, so I hadn't been working hands-on with the orangutans on a daily basis for a while. We decided to give Hsing Hsing and Puteri a bit of a break, so we separated them, knowing we could try Puteri again with Hsing in the future. When I started back on the orangutan round soon afterwards, I studied Puteri's records in more detail and realised that there had been a noticeable gap since Puteri's last proper menstruation. I tried not to get excited but decided to do a pregnancy test on her that day.

I brought Puteri inside and gave her about a litre of fluids to make her pee. Her bladder didn't weaken, so I gave her even more fluids to no avail. I swear she knew that I needed a sample. I had a chiropractor appointment during my lunch break, so I reluctantly let Puteri outside without a precious yellow sample. I remember Rosemary telling me that Puteri wouldn't urinate in the den when she knew her keeper wanted a urine sample. Puteri must have sensed my earlier desperation so I decided to play it ultra-cool in the afternoon when I brought her inside for her dinner.

I chatted away to Puteri as I gave her an extra-tasty dinner, and I tried to hide my Cheshire-cat grin when she finally peed. I put her enrichment outside and then let her into the exhibit. Puteri eagerly exited the den in her quest to obtain more food, so I locked her out for a few minutes while I collected a urine sample. I didn't want to get anybody else's hopes up, so I did the pregnancy test in private with pursed lips and shaking hands. I thought at the time that I would truly be a mess if I ever had to do my own pregnancy test, and I would probably have to ask one of the other orangutan keepers to do it for me. I was put out of my misery quickly, as the test came up with a positive result almost immediately. Sam, who was looking after the gibbon round that day, had just returned to the orangutan area in our little golf buggy after doing her afternoon feeds. I was a gibbering mess of excitement, and my Italian hands were flapping about all over the place as I waved the positive pregnancy test around in front of her. Sam and I proceeded to embrace and jump up and down in glee with this unexpected and amazing discovery. We decided to keep it quiet and do a second test in the morning to confirm the result. I did ring Marty that night while I was walking Cooper to let her know that we were probably going to be aunties again very soon!

I think the positive cross came up even quicker when we did the test again the following morning, and we were ecstatic. I hadn't told our supervisor Clare yet, so I took the test up with me to her office before the staff meeting at 8.00 am, closed her office door and put the positive pregnancy test on her desk. I soon found out that her resulting tense and wide-eyed facial expression was because she thought that the test belonged to me and that I was about to have a meltdown in her office before our staff meeting because I was pregnant! When I realised her bewilderment I blurted out, 'It's Puteri's!' and Clare seemed both happy and relieved.

Leif and I went in with Puteri the next day to try to confirm genital swelling, another sign of pregnancy. Puteri seemed to find our actions quite horrifying, and she would not let either one of us look at her private parts. If one of us tilted our head to try to have a look, she would turn the other way or sit firmly on the ground so nothing could be seen. I finally got a very quick peek and swelling was confirmed. We used to joke that Puteri always looked six months pregnant since she had always been a 'big boned' and plump orangutan. Now that Puteri was in fact pregnant, she had a legitimate excuse for being a bit fat!

I did the predicted birth-date calculations as best I could without having an exact conception date. The baby was due from mid-September to late October 2009, so Sam and I were stoked that Puteri didn't give birth while we were in Sumatra. On the morning of 20 October 2009, I saw that Puteri was in labour when I was giving out enrichment from the keeper roof. She was in some distress, as any woman is during labour. Unlike human females, who can ask for an epidural and crush their partner's hand, Puteri, like all female orangutans, gave birth alone and with minimal fuss. Orangutan labours are much quicker than those of human females, averaging a few hours or less. Orangutan babies are considerably smaller than human infants, generally weighing between 1.5 and 2 kilograms, and this contributes to a much easier and quicker labour for orangutan mothers.

I think orangutan babies are much cuter and quieter than their human counterparts. You will rarely hear a peep out of an orangutan baby, unlike the piercing screams often unleashed by newborn human babies. Also, unlike helpless human babies, orangutan babies grip onto their mother's hair immediately after birth, leaving the mother orangutan with her hands free so she can still climb through the canopy. I'm sure many human mothers wish their newborn babies had this ability so multitasking was still possible.

After giving birth in her outside exhibit, Puteri immediately began to cradle and clean her tiny infant. She also ate the placenta, which is normal behaviour for an orangutan female, as this provides vital energy and nutrients after the draining labour. Puteri showed how much she trusted her keepers as she quickly came inside to visit us at the mesh. Puteri eagerly took food and fluids from us while we fussed over the precious new arrival. Puteri was very protective of her newborn, and if the baby made a sound she would nuzzle and rock it, just as a human mother would. The baby appeared strong and alert, and we observed it suckling almost immediately. We confirmed that the baby was a girl the next day. We were all elated, since orangutan females are precious in captivity. One male orangutan can be used to mate with numerous females, so not as many are needed in captivity. Females are vital to ensure that the captive population can continue to grow. Of course we adore our two young male orangutans at the zoo, Semeru and Nyaru, but I had been praying for months that Puteri's infant would not have an extra appendage. It was sheer relief when we confirmed the new arrival was a little girl. It also meant that Hsing still had a 100 per cent success rate of siring females, with this being daughter number four.

Puteri's new baby daughter provided the perfect platform to launch the 'Don't Palm Us Off' campaign in November 2009. During this time, I was undertaking an Australian lecture tour on orangutan conservation with Dr Ian Singleton. As I was boarding a flight back home to Perth, I received a phone call from a Perth Zoo marketing staff member. They wanted to launch the campaign the following day by filming Leif and me doing a contact session with Puteri and her four-week-old baby. We were also going to have a naming competition for the baby. All of that seemed fine until I heard the question, 'Can you wear that T-shirt with the "Don't Palm Us Off" logo on it?' I responded with, 'Excuse me? Are you serious? I haven't even washed it since getting back home from Sumatra almost two months ago. Aggggghhhhhh'.

There was nothing I could do, since I wasn't getting home until that evening and I didn't have a clothes dryer. So I was just

218

going to have to locate and wear the foul-smelling, gross and unwashed skin-tight white T-shirt. It was bad enough wearing it in the jungle, but this time I had to wear it in front of TV cameras. After arriving home from the airport that night, I ventured into the laundry and tentatively dug to the bottom of the dirty-clothes basket. I found a plastic bag – the same plastic bag into which I had shoved the offending T-shirt after my stinky jungle trek to visit Temara. I peeled the T-shirt out of the bag, sprayed it with some perfume and hung it outside to air it as best I could.

The contact session with Puteri and bubs went well the next day, despite my revulsion at having to wear the rank and stinky T-shirt. Puteri spent most of her time with Leif, so perhaps she was also repulsed by my recycled attire. The name chosen for Puteri's baby had to begin with the letter 'T', just as Temara's name did.

Puteri cuddling Leif and avoiding stinky recycled jungle T-shirt

The orangutans at Perth Zoo all have Indonesian names, and our newest youngster was soon named Teliti, meaning 'to be careful and thorough' in Indonesian. This name was chosen to reflect Puteri's loving and careful mothering style.

Teliti was a gorgeous baby, but she had a cheeky glint in her eye from a very early age. I couldn't help but wonder if the torch had been passed and we had a mini Temara on our hands. This thought became eerily prophetic a couple of weeks later, when we had word from Sumatra that the trackers could not locate Temara. She had moved away from her tracker during a storm and despite an intensive week-long search there was no sign of her. Temara had eluded her trackers twice before for a few days at a time, but on both of those occasions she had made her way back to the station area and made herself known to staff. This time Temara had left the station area itself, so it appeared she had made the decision to move on and have some privacy after having had her every move watched for three years. I'm sure Temara would have been sitting well hidden in a tall tree as she watched the trackers searching for her from below and calling her name. She could have come down for food from the trackers, but the fruiting season was in full swing so she had a smorgasbord on hand.

I somehow knew deep down that they wouldn't find Temara — at least not in the near future. In a way I was glad she had cut the apron strings herself and moved away of her own accord. As her 'guardian', I would have found it very difficult to say, 'Yes, let's stop following her', but I was confident that, after having been followed for three years, Temara had the intelligence and the skills to survive on her own in her new jungle home. If anything, I think the trackers had been holding Temara back, and without them she would now be able to make the complete transition to jungle life. Temara had already demonstrated that even if an orangutan has never experienced life in the wild, if mentally and socially healthy, they can possess the skills, curiosity and intelligence to adapt to wild living with the appropriate support.

I was excited about the prospect of Temara locating an adult male orangutan to mate with, so she could contribute to the growing orangutan population in BTP. It was highly likely that Temara's hormones were leading the way to her new destination. I felt a great sense of peace and hope knowing that Temara had returned to the land from which her grandmother had been taken years before. Temara had left her old life far behind and she was now in charge of her own destiny.

22

The future

It has been numerous years since Temara was last seen in BTP. I often think about the roller-coaster ride we shared together as she adapted to her new jungle life. My thoughts will drift to Temara when I see cheeky Teliti behaving in a similar way to her older, strong-willed sister. Temara especially comes to mind when we are trying to fend off Teliti in contact sessions. Teliti is a biter! She bites our boots. She bites our keys. She bites our two-way radios. And she tries to bite us.

Puteri almost seems relieved when we visit them in the exhibit so she can have a break from her delinquent daughter. Puti tends to want to cuddle up with Martina while the other orangutan keeper and I become landing platforms for Teliti as she flings herself off the climbing poles and into our laps. If Teliti does become too rough, we beg Puteri for some assistance, since she is the only one who can control her hyperactive child. In saying that, Puteri is a

Having a play-wrestle with Teliti

far more relaxed mother than some of our other orangutans. They wouldn't let their children get away with such behaviour.

Every time I return to the jungles of BTP, I have a glimmer of hope that I may be lucky enough to see my fiery red-headed friend. The ultimate experience would be to see Temara with a baby and know that new life has entered the jungles from which Temara's grandparents were taken years ago. The staff at the release site always record orangutan sightings and take photos, so I hope that Temara's happy snap will appear one day.

Temara brought much publicity to the importance of the BTP ecosystem. People who had never heard of it were now intrigued and eager to hear news from this release site and aid in the protection of this habitat.

Being involved with Temara's release into the wild has been the highlight of my career. On a personal level, my time spent with Temara in the jungle was challenging and all-encompassing at times. To undertake such a bold and innovative project amid risk and harsh conditions was exhausting but worth every sleepless night, neck cramp, foot fungus, rash, bee sting and leech bite. I left Temara in her new jungle home, where each new day heralded an array of choices and experiences that a captive orangutan can never have. The observations and photographs taken of Temara during the three years she was followed show that she was succeeding in her adaptation to the wild. But more importantly to me, as her keeper and friend, I truly believe in my heart that Temara is happy, and that is all I ever wanted for her.

Temara living the jungle dream life (Photo: Peter Pratje)

IS THERE HOPE?

Mahatma Gandhi said, 'The greatness of a nation and its moral progress can be judged by the way its animals are treated'.

I sometimes feel a great melancholy at being part of the human species, a species that is capable of abhorrent cruelty, so often towards innocent animals that have no voice of their own. With exponential population growth and our increasing need for limited resources, the human species is quickly destroying the only known planet on which we can live. Tragically, it is our great ape cousins – chimpanzees, bonobos, orangutans and gorillas – that face imminent extinction at the hands of their supposedly more intelligent human counterparts.

I have witnessed first-hand the cruelty humans have inflicted on orangutans in Indonesia. It is truly heart-wrenching to look into the eyes of a traumatised orphan baby orangutan. No one can fully comprehend the sadness it experiences when its mother and natural way of life in the jungle are so cruelly stolen away. Their emotional scars cut even deeper than the physical scars that some bear from their capture.

The battle facing orangutans sometimes seems insurmountable, but just as I have witnessed the results of human cruelty towards orangutans, I have also seen people who are capable of great kindness and compassion, who have dedicated their lives to help prevent the extinction of this beautiful and intelligent species, who fight relentlessly against the companies that destroy the Indonesian rainforest to make a profit, who fight against the corruption that has infiltrated some of the very orangisations that should be protecting orangutan habitat. These people inspire me to carry on my fight to help save this precious species, to never give up, to always fight for the orangutans, because they need every voice that is prepared to speak for them.

But time is fast running out and the orangutan is sitting on a ticking time bomb. We need more help. I hope Temara's story and the urgent struggle facing orangutans will inspire you to also become a voice for our orange cousins. There are times when my heart will flitter with hope when I hear the voice of change – a seven-year-old child who proudly announces at my zoo orangutan presentation that they won't eat a certain chocolate bar because it contains palm oil. This is the change and passion the orangutans need, but sadly, it's not enough.

To be blunt, what we need to save the orangutan in the immediate future is money. Money to support conservation groups and on-the-ground projects that have a real impact on protecting wild orangutan populations and their habitat. Money to fight the foreign investors and corrupt people driving the relentless deforestation in Indonesia. If the forests of Indonesia continue to be ravaged as they are, then thousands of species will become extinct, including the Sumatran orangutan, sun bear, tiger and elephant. How can we as an 'intelligent' species allow this to happen?

I hope against all hope that the human species takes heed of this poignant and very relevant Native American saying, which epitomises why the orangutan is facing extinction:

> *When the last tree has been cut down, the last fish caught, the last river poisoned, only then will we realise that one cannot eat money.*

YES, YOU CAN HELP

The Orangutan Project (TOP) is an inspiring organisation. TOP works cooperatively with multiple stakeholders, both in Indonesia and Malaysia. This strategy has meant TOP being recognised worldwide as the premier orangutan conservation organisation. From humble beginnings, TOP now sends more than $1.4 million per annum to reputable orangutan conservation projects, with administration costs kept very low. More than $7 million dollars in total has been sent to fund various projects, including habitat protection, orangutan rescue teams, education programs, orangutan rescue centres and release programs, including the Sumatran orangutan release site at BTP.

Please visit The Orangutan Project's website – www.orangutan.org.au – to help us prevent the extinction of the orangutan. Protecting wild orangutan populations is the only way the species can be saved. You can become a TOP supporter, join an orangutan eco-tour, make a donation, adopt an orphaned orangutan, purchase palm-oil-free products and join the Palm Oil Resistance.

I will always be grateful that I'm able to work so closely with the Sumatran orangutans at Perth Zoo. Spending so much time with the Orange Kids has made me feel like they're members of my own family. I only have to spend a few seconds in the orangutan corridor to know what mood each orangutan is in. They have all touched my heart and I love them all dearly. A few of my orange friends hold an extra-special place in my heart, and Temara will always be one of those. I'm so proud that Perth Zoo had the courage and vision to support the release of Temara into the jungles of BTP. Perth Zoo has a strong commitment to conservation projects in the field, and financially assists the BTP orangutan release site.

Please visit the Perth Zoo website – www.perthzoo.wa.gov.au – to learn more about the Sumatran orangutan colony, and the conservation work with Australian native species and overseas projects to which the zoo contributes. You can make a donation to Wildlife Conservation Action, which supports the Bukit Tigipuluh release program.

I strongly encourage you to lead by example and be the change you want to see in the world. If everyone develops this attitude, then maybe, just maybe, we can bring the orangutan back from the looming precipice of extinction.

NOTES

1   N. Rowe, *The Pictorial Guide to the Living Primates*, Pogonias Press, New York, 1996.

2   Ibid.

3   C. Van Schaik, *Among Orangutans: Red Apes and the Rise of Human Culture*, Belknap Press, Cambridge, Massachusetts, 2004.

4   M. Leach, *The Great Apes: Our Face in Nature's Mirror*, Blandford Press, London, 1996.

5   I. MacKinnon 'Palm oil: the biofuel of the future driving an ecological disaster now', *The Guardian*, 4 April 2007, www.guardian.co.uk/environment/2007/apr/04/energy.indonesia

6   A. Pachter, 'Greenpeace opposing Neste palm-based biodiesel', *Epoch Times*, 12 October 2007, www.theepochtimes.com/news/7-10-12/60555.html.

7   'The Bukit Tigapuluh Landscape Conservation Programme', Frankfurt Zoological Society, www.fzs.org/en/projects-2/current-projects/bukit-tigapuluh.

8   B. Galdikas, 'Orangutans: Indonesia's "people of the forest"', *National Geographic*, vol. 148, no. 4, October 1975, pp. 444–73.

9   J. Goodall, *Reason for Hope: A Spiritual Journey*, Soko Publications and Phillip Berman, New York, 1999.

FURTHER READING

Cocks, Leif, *Orangutans and Their Battle for Survival*, University of Western Australia Publishing, Perth, 2002

Galdikas, Birute, 'Orangutans: Indonesia's "people of the forest"', *National Geographic*, vol. 148, no. 4, October 1975, pp. 444–73

Galdikas, Birute, M. F., *Reflections of Eden*, Back Bay Books: Little, Brown and Company, 1995

Goodall, Jane, *Reason for Hope: A Spiritual Journey*, Soko Publications and Phillip Berman, New York, 1999

Leach, Michael, *The Great Apes: Our Face in Nature's Mirror*, Blandford Press, London, 1996

Rowe, Noel, *The Pictorial Guide to the Living Primates*, Pogonias Press, New York, 1996

Van Schaik, Careel, *Among Orangutans: Red Apes and the Rise of Human Culture*, Belknap Press, Cambridge, Massachusetts, 2004

ACKNOWLEDGEMENTS

I would never have had the opportunity to write this book were it not for my orangutan mentor, Leif Cocks. I will always be thankful that he entrusted me to look after the Perth Zoo orangutans when I was so young and wide-eyed with sheer enthusiasm. His knowledge and passion for orangutans is inspirational, and his commitment to orangutan conservation is steadfast and unwavering. Leif had the vision and the courage to make the dream of a zoo-born orangutan being released into the wild a reality. I am honoured that I helped this dream become history in the making.

There were many who doubted whether a zoo-born orangutan could adapt to living in the wild. Thank you to the Perth Zoo management team and my fellow keepers for supporting and believing in Temara. As Nelson Mandela said, 'It always seems impossible until it's done.'

Thanks to my 'zoo girls' – we started out as work colleagues but they became some of my dearest friends in the world. Not only do we share a commitment to our animals and conservation, but we've shared some hilarious moments together. A bunch of zookeepers can manage to make poo and other gross things a part of normal lunchtime conversation. I don't know what I'd do without them and know that we'll be friends forever.

I am lucky to be one of those few people who have truly remarkable and supportive parents. They have been my rock and provided me with love, support, guidance and a stern lecture or pep talk if required. They have embraced my love of animals and passion for conservation, and are always there to help, whether it be looking after my pets while I'm traipsing through the jungle or assisting with an orangutan fundraiser. My parents have always encouraged me to follow my heart and my dreams and to strive for the top of that mountain, no matter how high and treacherous it may seem. A big thanks to my older brother, Michael, who has also always been so supportive of my orangutan work and a great big brother all round. He is always willing to use his photography and computer-geek skills to help me with the more technical side of my work for TOP.

A big thankyou to The Orangutan Project team with whom I work. We strive tirelessly to help prevent the extinction of the orangutan. Working with such dedicated and like-minded people gives me the strength to continue even when our goal sometimes seems out of reach.

And finally, thanks to Grant. We met after Temara had been released but he is so supportive and understanding when he comes second to my Orange Kids – as he often does. I need to thank him for being so accepting of my orangutan obsession and for understanding that our son, Logan, may become a 'tree-hugger' like his mum.